THE
ENDLESS
ABIDING

THE ENDLESS ABIDING

FIELD NOTES FROM THE JOURNEY WITHIN

JENNIFER PIRECKI

Redfern Ink
Franklin, Tennessee

Published by Redfern Ink
P O Box 1187
Franklin, Tennessee 37065

Copyright © 2025 by Jennifer Pirecki

All rights reserved. No part of this publication may be reproduced or transmitted in any form or by any means, electronic or mechanical, including photocopy, recording, or any information storage and retrieval system, without the prior written permission of the publisher.

Published in the United States of America

Cover Photos: Jennifer Pirecki
Cover Design: Dan Harding, Blue Mile Design
Interior Design: Andrea Reider

ISBN 978-0-9994690-9-5
ISBN 979-8-9921151-0-9 (e-book)

Library of Congress Control Number: 2024926307

1 3 5 7 9 10 8 6 4 2

First Edition

1. Spirituality 2. Personal Memoirs

CONTENTS

Before Beginning vii

Dearest Cousin 1

July 5

August 21

September 75

October 117

November 161

Three Years Later 187

Acknowledgments 193

Notes 197

BEFORE BEGINNING

20 / 20

One evening, while walking Totem in my neighborhood, caught up in weariness from wrestling against a bitter layer cake of reckonings that awaited me, I was struck by an earnest need to release some things in a more complete surrender.

After 19 fruitful years as a private practice psychotherapist, a marriage and family therapist to be exact, my faith consistently played a role in client engagement, though it had become diluted over time by the rubric of psychotherapy and its doctrines of self-care, self-help, and self-sufficiency. What stopped me in my tracks was the realization that I had subtly folded into a secular religion only to become a tenured member of its priestly class. While tacit acceptance is given to spiritual practices, a full-scale interweave of the Person, healing, and teaching of Jesus Christ as the resolution to our generational and individual need for God is marginalized as inferior to the metrics of psychotherapy. The soul as a vital form of created intelligence is sadly subjugated to the narrative of the brain's superiority.

That evening walk became an outpouring of contrition and heartfelt repentance for my unknowing participation in a religious system that once originated with the Healer, but had in large part disowned Him. My pledge was to speak of the True Author of health and healing to anyone He guided me. Given the immediate events to follow, I could never have anticipated the confirmation I would soon receive.

A worldwide pandemic utterly destabilized our human way of life just days after this personal surrender. Indeed, we had ever so slowly, under the cover of darkness careened into an iceberg, completely shocked by its immensity and devastation. Yet, for the most part, we were, and are still arranging deck chairs. Some among us are broken beyond repair, longing for the comforts of our past, as we continue to betray ourselves in ways we must deny in order to survive the onslaught of pervasive desecration. Exposure to the reality of our culpability in our own demise may hold consequences that are just too much to bear.

In the midst of this crisis, many healing practitioners muted their role as conduits of guidance and solace in the face of extraordinary trauma, which sharpened my resolve to step into the void in my own small way, to be available and physically present to speak of the healing power of Jesus Christ as clearly and lovingly as possible with the hope that each living soul I encountered might endeavor to access their innermost chamber where their Maker desires to reside. For that is, and has always been, all we really have. And this remains humanity's most underdeveloped terrain.

Our collective reckonings as a species tragically continue. Our misplaced generational allegiances to corrupt constructs have woefully imprisoned us spiritually while cleverly separating us from our souls and our God. We have arrived at a crossroads as the precipice to further disintegration fast approaches. An alternate path forward demands a personal and complete surrender to the Beyond Within. Only a full yielding to His will and design for our lives will guide us through our uncertain future, having become blinded by the comforts and promises of all sorts of false religions. The door to our liberation is unlocked by the Key Within who removes any barrier to our living souls' communion with the Most High God who made them. A restoring of our inner lands must come before the larger restoration can begin, as ongoing upheaval shows us where we really are on our inner journey: we are lost prodigals who need to come to our senses, humble ourselves, and return home. Our Father remembers our frame, He remembers that we are but dust and welcomes us with a love beyond imagining. Yet we are so willfully wayward. What else is needed to awaken us from our slumber? The time for lingering in our denial and apathy has long come to a close.

Truth is the only antidote for our terminal disease; its eternal Light upon each soul the only Agent to eradicate the layers of internal decay. What is Truth? A simpler question: *Who* is Truth? He who hung upon wooden planks driven into a parched land long ago so that we might become free from our inner planks, some constructed by our own hands, some inherited from an ages-old generational lineage. It is through this contextual backdrop that the invitation from The Endless Abiding urgently makes Itself known to us all.

The Abiding Principal

This volume of field notes is a short-handed recording of The Abiding Principal's revealing to one soul in real time as these cultural shifts unfolded. While always a deepening mystery, The Endless Abiding, as I have come to understand in part, is a regenerative and sustaining state of being within and against the wounding of our times, tethering us eternally while expressing Itself temporally.

As innumerable resources verify, to practice a habit as a form until a preferred behavior takes its place is a necessary effort. Passive actions such as movement in nature, observation, inquiry, and examination of the intricate communication between the external and internal landscapes, with a persistent curiosity towards any blockage to The Abiding Principal's potential in my soul as His vessel, effectively reinforced this daily practice. Tracing the life and way of Jesus Christ in the pages of the Gospels continually drew this seeker's attention to the interrelationship between His Person, His healings, and His teachings as the framework for my being and believing. Though challenging to understand when the soul's eye is obstructed by unhealed material, the more I joined with my Inner Field's plowing and turning over, the more my understanding and connection increased in concert with whatever healing was transpiring. Tending any field over time is a long and loving labor with seasons of harsh weather and abundant harvests. I do my best to depict this creative process that, in my experience, has a sublime logic of its own, personalized to the contours and features of each seeker's Inner Field.

My caution to anyone desiring a deeper experience of The Endless Abiding in the hopes that their pains might be avoided: these *very* pains comprise the highly unique path to your transformation and union with God. The pursuit of the practice without an awareness of what The Abiding Principal will do with your receptive vessel would exchange a renewing communion for a superficial intimacy. The untold benefit of your willingness to be the clay in the Potter's hands is your soul's complete healing unto wholeness as He painstakingly strengthens your vessel to hold the loving and fulfilling Substance from which His purposes will emerge. However, be forewarned, the healing of deeply rooted wounds comes first as I can attest.

At the root of my unhealed wounds was this core reckoning: my relationship to God had been significantly marred by a toxic blend of internalized family dysfunction and its seamless enmeshment with the religious construct of the church. The resulting default programs and their crippling effects remained unchallenged by my anemic connection with Jesus Christ and to His Spirit. In order to begin a new season of painful healing, an exit from these dynamics was necessary, especially due to the problematic role I had played in them for so long. These departures secured the loss of many dreams of what my life might look like some day, the very aftermath I had worked so hard to avoid. As I believed these issues had been previously resolved during my therapeutic journey facilitated by exceptional helpers, I was at first quite overwhelmed that the Healer's initial survey determined these mounting losses were to be cleared from my Inner Field before Abiding could become possible.

When my inner ears were clogged and I could not hear or listen well, The Abiding Principal would make Himself known through His Word, which I would carry along with my notebook on every field walk and read during my garden pause. No matter the impact of man's mishandling of the Bible, in a natural setting, from a surrendered pose, its pages illuminate our human condition and our generational need for God to serve as a mirror. As such, it magnifies far more than we ever want to see about ourselves, but need so desperately to heal and live. We are prone to swim in the surface waters of devotions while we are here to learn how to breathe under water in devotion to our Savior-Brother-Friend and all He deeply wants to share with us about our Father, often through His timeless Word and the wealth of inner dialogues published by our forebears therein.

Suggestions for Reading

You are welcome to eavesdrop on these unfiltered inner conversations recorded during the garden pauses that followed my daily field walks. Each day my Inner Field was softened, loosened, and cleared of debris that inhibited life with my Father in some way. While resolution to my concerns would come in Another's timing, His frequent encouragement to me was to rest and return in order to receive the spiritual nourishment available through the unending interaction between the natural setting without, His Word, and the landscape within. You will notice incomplete notes at the end of most entries; these are often paraphrased Bible verses from *Daily Light for Every Day*, or lines from Henri Nouwen's *Inner Voice of Love*, which traveled with me to the garden. Occasionally, anecdotal musings or phrases from *Reckoning With Dust* and *Anthroprose* were brought to mind with new insights for my growing understanding of the reckonings I was living through. Stanzas of hymns from my youth also emerged to both sing as I walked and note in writing. As my cousin was the first reader of this collection, I begin with the letter addressed to him as it introduces many of the lessons I was learning at the time.

Totem, my Rhodesian Ridgeback and faithful companion, accompanied me every day to our sacred field. You will see he mentors me in the realm of the sensory and language of the soul. His movement and demeanor amongst Field's creatures taught me immeasurably more than this volume captures.

Patiently waiting on The Abiding Principal's pace is essential to the continuing dialogue, as I have found His methods to be deliberate, extremely thorough, much of the time hidden, and exceedingly kind. It is only when I review weeks and months of field notes that I see the Master Embroiderer's gracious hand tenderly untangling and stitching together every thread of my human frailty. As these entries were written over a period of months, they are most suitable for unhurried reading and prayerful introspection. My hope in sharing them with you is that your seeking soul might find your Inner Field where The Endless Abiding longs to be found.

THE ENDLESS ABIDING

March 14, 2022

Dearest Cousin,

As I have drafted these entries for the last little while, I am unsure of what you will see in them or think of them. But I am pleased to share them with you.

Taken directly from several notebooks filled during daily visits to my writing hideaway, this collection of field notes was recorded over approximately four months—16 months into the existential turbulence we now call a pandemic.

Hour by hour, day by day, throughout this changing season, the soul hunger of each and every client-seeker, including my own, makes itself known. It is clear that numerous narratives we foreclose upon only feed our souls' distress, as constructs we have once trusted refuse to come to the table with any sustaining nourishment. We are starving for an incorruptible food.

How do we live through such a time without asking these questions:

What am I here to heal? What am I here to learn?

In addition to other queries bumping around in the basement of our being:

Is there a God? Does He care about me? If so, is there a unique purpose that only I can express through this gift of Life?

Many claim a faith that has been severely tested by these times, and frankly, I find helpful resources lacking for how to move forward from here. Presently, there is a scrambling afoot to generate answers for our disaffected culture in turmoil from a reactionary posture. Whatever comes of these efforts will also likely prove dissatisfying to the soul, as we are a traumatized people in desperate need of spiritual healing.

Traversing the inner spiritual path is all that matters now; it is the way to that healing. Additionally, Jesus Christ is more essential than ever and even less known by those who claim Him as the Hinge upon Whom their faith depends. Many seekers are surprised to hear Him so plainly named in the therapy space as *Healthy-Human-Healer-Hero* (and so much more) who changed the course of *history*, while we may only agree upon the reality that the calendar was zeroed out by His appearance on the scene. Yet, as most religions have to address Him in some way, my bias holds: *He is* the Beginning and the End of this age and we are reckoning with what that means on our souls' level. Unfortunately, abundant distractions continue to hijack our precious attention away from the inward journey to the soul, the innermost vessel of our created spiritual nature. This is sufficient evidence that our personal connection to The Beyond Within through our soul and spirit, and yes, the *Real* Jesus Christ, is far more potent than any narrative or projected outcome.

My sincere hope is that these daily attempts to yield to That Which Sustains during unthinkable times will encourage those who feel disconnected from The Beyond Within to insistently pursue and record their own Inner Field work. *That they would sell all they have, buy the Field where their Treasure lies hidden, and devote themselves to*

Its reclamation. The greater hope is that somehow, as each individual chooses this pilgrimage of Truth for themselves, and then nurtures and tends it, together we may break through this watershed existential moment by that power and peace which will inevitably result for the individual, thereby transforming our collective human family. *For vibrant inner Communion could only convert to a changed Community.*

In addition to anything I have already conveyed, the capitalization of the characters may get under your skin: *You, Field, Herd, Hawk, Garden, Osage Orange, Treasure, Sun,* attributes of *You.* This is purposeful if distracting. So little is truly sacrosanct anymore. This is my small stand.

Though characteristic of field notes, any half thoughts, run-on sentences, fragments, italicized phrasing, and repeated words might frustrate your literary sensibilities. If these imperfections reflect that there is no command of language needed to explore the terrain of the Inner Field, I am happy for it.

When I reread this volume, I sometimes wonder, *are you sure that this was what you were experiencing?* I quickly answer myself: *Yes, you know this absolutely; it is why you are more peaceful and contented than you have ever been.* I also know that when the wintery gaps in my Field walks and Garden pauses arrive, the disconnection slips right back in and becomes the greater reality, and it is this perpetual surfacing of disconnect that causes me to question. When I go to the Field, and then the Garden, the question evaporates, for my soul's memory is greater than any question. It reminds me that I have found the Treasure buried there and It waits for me still.

JULY

July 25
Sunday

I am at home here, in this Field. Although, it is not mine. I do not own it; it is but a transitory base of operations, where I am more trespasser than steward.

This sacred sanctuary, this parish fellowship is where I come to commune with Our Creator, alongside other creature congregants.

The crows offer their invocation as I write. Likely, they noisily gather to flush out a hawk that threatens them. This Sunday morning, the quietest of the week, their *caw caw cawing* breaks the silence with what I have come to expect and understand, at least in part.

I could say that I found this Field approximately five years ago, but that would be a half-truth. It wooed me until I responded. A layer cake of reckonings played its role in the wooing, as a long season of beginnings and endings demanded living through.

One layer: I had knowingly taken the posture of persona non grata in my family. To become its exile was an enormous departure for me, and the sudden movements reduced my scaffolding-of-a-self to a tangled heap, rendering hopeful dreams of connection beyond recovery. This is why I held on as long as I did. Some part of me knew the undoing would never be undone. It was *good-bye for now*, a much-misunderstood adieu. And this was only one layer of the cake to be consumed.

It has dawned on me to start here for many reasons. Mostly, I feel prompting that I understand now to be

Inspiration knocking at my heart's door, urging me to stop thinking and just *write*.

On this warmest and most humid of July mornings, I pen this attempt at a beginning. And an end, in that the threads desiring to be woven into the larger tapestry of my life are hindsightings left hanging loose for long enough. Writing chronicles, but also carries forward my own integration, and then, foreshadows what is next for the undulating movements of my lightened soul, more unburdened.

I have a few places to write; quiet nooks with books and beautiful light. Yet, I choose this place now because nothing compares to how I feel when I am here.

I sit under the Garden's towering Osage Orange tree, which is the Field's centerpiece and my witness, deeply rooted in Garden's lawn. It often serves as a pulpit-perch for the hawk or the vulture. Lately, they take their place in the neighboring cedar or the maple that borders the graveyard. When the hay rounds are available to them, the hawks are kind to show their grandeur at eye level. I am saddened on the day I see the rounds shuffled to the side, reminding me of the constancy of change which will not be denied and presses us all forward.

A woodpecker types away over my left shoulder. The burl on the Osage Orange is over my right. Only today, after five years of marveling at it, do I see its magnificence as the largest heart I have ever seen. As happens here almost daily, I realize it has been waiting for me all along, for me to see it for what it is. Perhaps it will help me open my own heart upon these pages, or give me courage to write what I must write, despite the heartbreak of it all. Yet, I have written before from my Heart of hearts, and I know it is the only place I feel most alive. Writing from anywhere else seems like a fool's errand, or heresy. I must come from here.

At once, I hear the voices of others who know of and come to this precious spot as well. At once, my worst nature shows itself. I do not want to share what is *mine*. But, of course, that is the whole point; this Field will never be mine, I shall never possess it. Ownership would spoil what I receive here—the experience of Home within, which belongs to The Endless Abiding.

July 26

The air can be so heavy, laden with moisture.
Who knew a person could suffocate by this Tennessee humidity?

You were the only One who traveled with me, my only Companion. For all of the religion of my upbringing, this Friendship is what my soul longed for but found missing within the constructs of church and family, which, for me, were interchangeable. Hence, the destruction, the demise. These were never satisfying, being instead illusions and delusions. In some ways, I am still deprogramming my operating system from the facsimiles of faith imprinted upon my cellular understanding of You from the confusing blend of church and family systems. It takes time to find freedom from this tangled prison. The web is sticky. I desperately wipe it off here, only to catch myself in it there. And so it goes.

I think I have come to know over the course of recent years that following You is a zero-sum game, requiring everything. No holding back, total surrender, and then the waiting…and more waiting…

Only through the microscope of hindsight can I understand more about this arduous season, and about *Reckoning*. This bless*ed* Field helps me grapple with whatever You bring to mind and heart day after day. I am a willing participant in this continual work in progress. I have agreed to it.

What remains a solid touchstone, a place to return when confused, is further inquiry regarding what impedes Your infilling of me. It also feels or seems safe to propose that if You were actively about anything, You were and are about interlinking faith in You and inner healing. My belief in this, in You, was the threshold that needed crossing. You know intimately what gets in my way, what obstacles are my unfinished business, what planks clutter my soul.

In a blink of an eye, access to Your Ultimate Healing Power is available. Yet integrating that Beyond by receiving Your Fullness Within, and _then_ yielding to *Your* living throughout everything that is the dailyness of my life as You transform me all the while; this becomes its own layer cake of challenge. If met solely on my own power or knowledge, I wouldn't even know how to begin this formidable pilgrimage.

Grace upon grace, the air is lighter as the cicadas sing from the cedars. The Sun's light vibrates their bellies and they share their frequency. They can't help it. They are noisy and unashamed to claim their Source of movement. They purify the air; their 17-year service to all has begun.

It seems the same with You; Your vibration cleansed this atmosphere, allowing us to breathe again.

Thank you, cicadas.

Thank you, Jesus.

salvation = soteria = breathe freely

July 27

From my Father:

You must write about the things you do not want to.
The very things.
What you have been avoiding.
The soul-aching pain that surfaces with the words.
The sorrow: 'This is not how it should be'.
But, it is what is.
The bottom of your abyss.

To acknowledge this fully, to not shrink back,
to know Who is using these very things
to restore the Wholeness you so badly desire,
while you assist others to retrieve It for themselves.
There is no way around, only through.
Your Wholeness must come first.

How can you share your story without reinjury to others?
Further scrutiny, judgment, misunderstanding?
Even with the greatest of care, some of this might occur,
but I will guide you if you yield even more
I will help you even with this.

These parts of you keep you veiled
in ways that no longer work.
No longer for Me, nor for you.
It seems you want to keep deepening these,

*your black marks in the shadows
while they frame the doorway to further emancipation,
and liberation for your soul.
It is your truth, but not your truth alone.*

*I was there with you as you struggled, wept, held, braced,
wearied yourself to the point that you had nothing left
for the things I wanted you to Be and do.
Yes, a choice was foist upon you at a crossroads of no return,
and looking back will be painful at first,
but a more complete understanding will come through the remembering,
and it will be useful.
Even more than it already has been useful.
Use is not your responsibility.
I Am responsible for use.
You are responsible to Me to speak the Truth as I guide you.
There, there is Fullness, there is Joy.
I Am Good.
You are Loved.*

～

When was the last time I saw my mother?

Approaching six years ago at the time of this writing. She seemed oblivious, even happy. Her best friend, my chosen Aunt, had come to town to help her pack.

I knew of her move, the sale of her home, the last place I saw my father alive. My spontaneous visit came on the heels of a job-loss notification, which thrust me into a new whirlwind of crisis. Yet, my Aunt's warm, steady presence gave me the courage to make my appearance.

My mother sat next to me on the green couch and then moved to the chair across from me. She wanted to face me. Our conversation was casual; yet, I remained guarded while resisting the urgency to flee. My Aunt calmed with her intermittent insertions of small talk; such relief those moments were.

It is clearer to me now that even then my mother was contending with cognitive changes, which were elusive and challenging to pin down given her personality and her usual behavior towards me. In some ways, this is also a relief, as any damage done, while still painful, seemed without malicious thought or intention. This allows for greater compassion today even if a confusing trend at the time. Her unknowing infliction of pain was not really new, but the diminished hope that my mother would ever learn to keep herself from inflicting pain was. The foregone conclusion was that she wouldn't be able to help herself. This only strengthened my resolve to set aflame the bridge between us, severing our tether.

I remember my Aunt comforting me outside as I prepared to leave. She applied kindness to my raw and shaken self; such a gift that she could stand in the gap for my mother, once again. For much of my life, she was the mother I longed for anyway. She now also stood in the gap for this one-time dutiful daughter whose former self would have relished the heroism and resented the martyrdom that were the inevitable rewards for this forced march. By her fidelity to my mother, a tribute to their lifelong friendship, she secured my release, leaving me to navigate the sharp edges of my siblings' contempt; indeed, they were unhappy with my disruptive exit.

While tearfully collapsing into her familiar pink top, I buckled under the weight of yet another fissure in my family's fracturing. Somehow, standing within my Aunt's embrace near the river birch, I knew this to be a final goodbye to many things; she wore the grace to bear it witness, for which I am forever in her debt.

July 30

I tend a colony of cats with food and water and love. They have varying temperaments; most are cagey and particular and hesitant to draw close no matter how much love I emit. In fact, they often run from me until they are hungry. Then they must abide enough in my presence and ask, often without sound, but maybe with just the blink of an eye. Trying too hard never helps.

This morning, Your Sun is a rose-gold orb. The mist lies like a cloak upon the Field. The openings between the cedars You fill with pockets of treasure, this rose-gold rarity. How blessed is the one who is able to see this.

A surprise trio of hawks appears to this observer who is convinced there exists only a duo. Perhaps all along what I thought was two was three.

One flies from the border of the Field, from the graveyard's maple, to the other. It swoops and circles, darting in and out of the canopy to ward off the cacophony of crows badgering the third hawk. Once successful in dodging the crows' sharp beaks and certain the previous victim has found safe harbor, it moves on to the Osage Orange to hold vigil in the Garden.

These mornings, my selfishness surfaces—my own inner crow. It taunts me relentlessly, not unlike the other visitors to *my* precious spot do.

Then, I feel like the hawk: *Can't you leave me in peace? I want to stay in this quiet just a moment longer.*

But that is not possible today. It's time to move on and refuse the crow its way, but I must outmaneuver it first—to keep it from following me to the next treetop.

trying → relying
hiding → abiding

July 31

Totem Talk:
Gentle
Down
Stay with me
Easy
Careful now

Sometimes I imagine I will shortcut our walk and choose to stay on the gravel drive that borders the Field. As I write, I have a broken toe and am unfamiliar with how it hinders one's gait. I think I will make it easier on Totem, my four-legged watchman, if I take this detour. Or, I won't get my feet wet if I stay on the border of the Field—I won't miss anything. This is what I tell myself.

This is utter heresy. I must be *in* the Field to experience the Field. Yes, every single day, my feet will get wet and I may come home with ticks on them. Even on the driest of days, when I am convinced there can be no dew, I find myself completely drenched, and I understand more what it means to consider the lilies and blades of grass.

It is a hazy, humid, last day of July. Yet, it feels tens of degrees cooler here. The cardinals are conversing with their chirping chatter near the crepe myrtles in full bloom. They overshadow the bank of white hydrangeas—the ones that inspired me to find the very hybrid for my own back yard.

Entering the Garden prior to walking the Field entirely feels like cheating. *The Field is the Way to the Garden.* As I am writing here for the time being, I can push myself to get here more quickly because *I must write*, but this spoils everything. Bordering the Field is not sufficient, I must enter in. *The vessel must be emptied to be filled with the Connection that inspires.*

Totem guards. He watches. His whiskers brush my arm like a butterfly's wings. A finch watches me from the top of the Garden's cedar, scarred by a breakage, or windstorm, or lightning bolt. It still stands tall, and I can smell it from here, even without a breeze. But perhaps I am able to receive the fragrance because I have done my due diligence and walked the Field. The inside of the cup has been cleaned.

While I have been flailing about in most things, I sense some consolidation centering on the obvious. Spiritual healing yields to The Potter's wheel in perpetual motion, which propels one towards wholeness, completion, freedom. Of late, I have come to understand more that there is no destination on this side of things. This movement on the inner healing → wholeness journey is it. The paradox: restful periods of stillness, of quiet introspection exist within the movement. They indeed are fuel for it, but also allow for His thorough assessment of the vessel's soundness. *What about the vessel needs tending, reshaping or mending? Does a new season require repair to continue with the fluid movement of Life-living?* These inquiries can surface during these interludes. At least that's what I think I know for now.

When I cannot see exactly where I am while The Potter's wheel turns, I decide to get my feet wet fully to remind myself that He Who generates the motion illuminates my path without me ever needing to know *where* I am exactly.

That knowledge becomes unimportant when He blankets me in coolness on the hottest of days, while He conducts a concert with the choir of birds eager to sing their morning love songs to their Maker.

Settle in.

May the God of all grace, who called us to His eternal glory by Christ Jesus, after you have suffered awhile, perfect, establish, strengthen and settle you.

To you who fear My Name the Sun of Righteousness shall arise with Healing in His wings and you shall go out and grow fat like stall-fed calves.

AUGUST

August 1

An August Prayer

With mind and heart, I say a prayer for an August abiding—and beyond.

I pray for many things, yet, somehow, I wonder if I ever unknowingly ask for a bonding to elements that do not serve me and are not in my best interest as Your child. These necessaries of life consume our sense of self to our detriment. They are fraudulences of Your unmatched Infinitude.

Your Inspiration is beckoning me to release those things which no longer belong. The familiar patterns and habits lurk and then pounce. Particularly when boredom or fatigue make themselves known. *All I have needed Thy hand hath provided. Blessings all mine with ten thousand beside.* A surplus, a feast, no lacking, no scrimping, no hedging.

Often I create hard and fast guidelines in hopes of purging these default patterns. You have helped me, empowered me to tackle much. Yet, I hold in reserve my want in the small and sneaky ways. I set a boundary, then flex the boundary. I disappoint myself. None of this works.

Would You fill me to the brim each day as a fattened calf? Would You allow me to experience it fully within my being? Would You satisfy my hunger in such a way that that want, and the time wanting, would be harnessed and utilized for You? Even in the simple but profound joy inexpressible of knowing You and communing with You. I would ask for a fresh revealing of You in these ways.

Thank You that it is Your will and desire for me to know this about You.

I will abide.

Let me lay aside every weight, and the sin, which so easily ensnares, and run with endurance the race set before me.

God has not given me a Spirit of fear but of power and love and a sound mind. Therefore, I will not be ashamed of the testimony of my Lord.

August 3

The dew is heavy upon the Field and Garden on this coolest of August mornings, which is an oxymoron. I survey the Garden after our walk through the Field and the grassy patch under Osage Orange calls to me. It might be the only dry place in the whole Field. The cardinals whoop their trilling in concert with our arrival. Their call-and-response is unmistakable. We are protected from view by a bank of hydrangeas, which has become my favorite specimen. Their prolific blooms are now a limey-brown foreshadowing of Fall.

Sally the beagle bays in the distance. She can be heard for miles away. Her voice is strong. The crickets are struggling to warm themselves with this coolness, their legs heavy with dew. Even with the brilliant Sun rising they silently complain that it is not warm enough to sing.

Totem, as always, is alert and watchful. Others may be walking the Field as we hide away for these precious moments. Sometimes the birdsongs sound like human whistles and he cocks his head in confusion.

The tree before me has seen everything. It has three hearty trunks spiraling outward and its branches do the same, spiraling out into infinity to catch the Sun's light, the dew, the birds. One can't help but feel protected by its majesty and spread. It anchors the rest here.

It often takes me until I reach the path lined by the cedars to feel attuned. By then, I have walked some, breathed some, and prayed more. I try to gaze at Sun until my eyes can take it no longer. The brilliance is far too much to bear.

The cedars form a tunnel-like portal. Each end of the path is a window to a different vista. I often place You before me and imagine You are walking ahead of me with the symphony of sounds and scents made all the more alive by Your Presence and Your Passing. Even the rocks cry out; they know Who You are, their Creator.

In this imaginary scene, I know I can't keep pace with You, and I leave room knowing others will seek You out for healing as I have. My healing, while not complete, has been undertaken.

This contented traveling does not require much of me, and I enjoy the breezes of Spirit that emanate from Your cloak and enshroud You.

A former imagining was the Hemorrhaging Woman and how she, in her exhausted, bloody state would have embarked upon her approach of You. My desperate exhaustion was my link to her. But now, things seem more peaceful. A space has been cleared as I have requested. So the struggle seems different now. To receive the gifts without bracing against, to allow the unworth to surface and be converted by the light of love that is this Bright Morning Sun.

How to thank You for this?

Your lovingkindness is everlasting. I declare it.

August 8
Sunday

And now, the quietude of a Sunday morning, infused with the bluebird's song, the blue jay's jeers, and the sweeping, lilting flight of the butterfly. The sonic undertow of the cricket's pitch; their frequency, if one will listen, is soul attuning.

We are often alone on Sundays, my favorite day to be here. Chickadees gather in the cedar before me which serves as a rehearsal stage for the birds in the Garden; even the hummingbirds perch to warm up their wings. A bee filters through like a cello's mellow drone. Totem eats grass around the base of Osage Orange before he thinks about settling in next to me. He sniffs my knee, then the page. He sits and then sniffs my face in question: *Will we be awhile?*

I haven't written for a few days. When I step away, I doubt there is anything worthwhile here. And, it has been a tumultuous week. My own soul clog reveals itself in a fresh way. My father's copy of Henri Nouwen's *Inner Voice of Love*, which I gave him 22 years ago, has returned to me. I reread the inscription. Although written to him, it delivers a timely message from my younger self across the decades, further exposing the hidden, painful need, with its tight-fisted grip on the back of my throat. Maybe this is why all I can do is exhale.

My therapist kindly but firmly places the lens of hindsight squarely upon my father. It's typical of me to venerate him and denigrate my mother. His need, too, was insatiable. I am sure my mother was relieved to have someone to share the load of his intensity, drive and expectation.

Somehow she seemed to use You to shield herself, but she never pulled me behind the shield with her; I was left to fend for myself.

It was too easy. I looked like him *at least I had his eyes*. I was his firstborn, as he was his father's. I was eager to please and perform for him. He would yell *Alaska*, and I would answer *Juneau*. He would inhale and I would exhale *maybe <u>this</u> is why all I can do is exhale*. To near perfection I became viscous mortar to his marriage as he was to his parents'. Indeed, our fusion started imperceptibly and early.

My mother always seems peripheral in memory, a non-interventionist. She would come behind his criticism and try to soften its edges, translating projected underlying feelings of love for me. So began the blending of love and comfort and performance and expectation. It was the currency of our connection for the majority of life. It would break him, eventually, as it has, and is, breaking me.

I can say that I am grateful to break differently. My breakage is gradual and inward. His was an explosive outwardness that ravaged us all. In many ways, those left in his wake have not, and might not, ever fully recover.

In the South, Brown Recluse spiders are a common nuisance. For the first time in 30 years of living within a five-mile radius of where I sit now, they have found us out and we must respond. A sorting and sifting through a lifetime of collected contents has ensued. All of his books, what remains of my father, are before me again. His notes, his handwriting. Receipts of purchase. There is more to unpack. I can see him so clearly in all of it. His best self—he became that at work, in his study, at the church. True to form, I have followed suit, less to avoid my marriage, more to avoid or to find myself.

These are the things that are changing now, as the secret pests of my inner being show themselves for the first time in awhile. At least to me. It's time. Beyond time.

Sun rises high enough to warm the cicadas into their vibration which initiates the benediction for today. I will be back.

August 9

Totem is growing more familiar with this new routine, our Garden diversion, with his blanket spread under Osage Orange. He is eager to move on, or guard. He is pleased that I bring him water in a familiar bowl. He drinks, he is thirsty. But this sturdy creature never complains.

He can't help his restless energy. His hound's senses pick up everything and he's always overstimulated. He just wants a scratch, a kiss, a treat. A place next to me. He guards to perfection.

He has warmly accepted our rescue cats who hold affection for him even with their aloofness. Another adjustment for him. He continues to flex and adapt as he approaches 11 years with us.

The crow caws from the very top of the cedar spire to another crow nearby. The Sun is veiled by our typical August haze.

Broken cisterns that hold no water leaps off the page at me while Totem settles. After sorting through many forgotten lifetimes of contents and images, I am processing the meticulous perfection by which I chronicled my achievements. Every ribbon, every certificate has been kept and stored. To a large degree, their condition is more pristine than photos of my graduations, my wedding. Those I obviously did not care as much about. The heat has rippled their plastic sleeves and curled the images. I am more inclined to set those aside, more drawn to the achievements noted. Or, really, I am taken by the perfection with which I have kept the results of those achievements.

Hence, I hold no water now. The cracks in my being keep manifesting the vessel's lack of soundness. There is no eternity in the ego. How sad when the masquerade deceives for so long.

I found a pre-wedding note written by my then soon-to-be husband. At first, I don't recognize its playful sweetness, mostly due to the brittleness of my calloused soul, worn and weathered by its overexposure to the egoic elements of my being and life itself. She demands recognition as the *One* who has done everything and been everything and followed obediently, heroically, and feels the reward is paltry. This is where Jonah comes from.

Cautionary, Jonah's book ends abruptly. Jesus comes to correct the record, and I am meant to fall in line behind His fullness and grace upon grace. My ego *thinks* she has, that's the problem with the Grand Deceit. So subtle, so conniving.

The Red-tailed Hawk left me a most beautiful feather this morning. Its auburn brilliance is the same shade as Totem's coat. Upturned and sitting on a piece of litter, it's an easily overlooked pointer. This paradox of flight and grounding; the debris discarded in the wrong place holds me back within and without.

The breeze blows carrying yet another paradox. The person in flight is not to be weighted down by successes and achievements of the world, which my hero self too eagerly craves. What tragedy to bind the eternal to the temporal. What grief once discovered.

I pray for quick conversion now. A translation of these insights into the dailyness of life. I want to soften. Yet, I believe You must heal my cracks first with the mortar of Your love for me. My soul knows this, and it's time I fall in line.

If anyone thirsts let him come to Me and drink.

August 10

I am late today and I forgot my glasses. The air is heavier each day.

Totem stands behind me drenched by dew. The Herd graced us with an appearance as we approached Amen Corner. Totem ventured halfway in to head them off at the crest in the middle of the Field. The momentary standoff is followed by a stampede of hind-footed beauty. Perhaps that is what kept him from chasing this time. These days he is a tad more careful as the thick brush is high and wet.

My fears creep in and resist my own progress. Fitful sleep is unusual for me. The new things taking shape need room; the fear wants to grip and remains tightly clenched. It feels like new effort to pry fear's bony fingers off of whatever it decides to clutch as it is being moved towards the exit door of my soul. The power of love, and a sound mind will only increase as I continue to stay current and sort my unfinished business. So I hope. I can see the fear thinking it can protect me from my not-enough self, my exiled daughter, the scapegoated hero with her shame, her festering wounds.

The few times I have been upended in this Field have come directly from the folly of a clutching grasp upon a force of nature that is Totem in prey drive. A few moments ago, I decided against holding him back from the chase, but instead to release him to his instincts:

This should be interesting; it is rare to see this ever-expanding Herd this late in the morning as Sun renders a golden hue to the Field's crest in stark contrast to the verdant shade of Amen Corner. No panic this time, no bracing, prayerful release: protect him, Lord Jesus, because there are at least two bucks among them, and Totem is older now.

The lead female takes her family away from Totem after her quick assessment, and the rest follow swiftly with her spotted fawn in the rear and we are treated to a passage that means more than my brain can process.

Striving feels heavy, like this blanket of heavy air, always fear-laden. The infinite perfection and completion of Your Presence in swiftness is far from that heaviness. The bracing, holding, constraining of what is Unlimited is not possible. Attempts will, and have, broken me.

The cedar is alive with the fluttering of finches. A woodpecker comes and goes. The breeze lifts the heaviness. The work of You, it is not mine to do. Help me to yield to it.

May I join the hind-footed Herd, even if I take up the rear, since it is new and unknown. You lead, I follow, no more grasping at wind.

We run together now
I in You
You in Me
We are one

August 11

Time feels compressed today. It isn't. I feel irritated, tense. The Field is always coolest at its center; the periphery is where I feel the heaviest. Breathing remains a chore on these most humid days of August.

I write these contemplations, which seem frivolous, against the backdrop of a cultural unraveling, as the crows gather at the far end of the Field. I have unearthed and unboxed books that I have carried with me for too many years. They reveal why. *Totem just now lies down, his backside against my hip, so I must be on target.*

In these books, I see where I left off, he left off, and the loose threads of gossamer that have been ignored for too long for the clutching I have chosen. What seems to be disclosing itself is the subtle way I shape-shifted my default programming and blended my vocation with it. My practice has become the primary field of play. It masquerades itself to me as ministry. Yet, that is where all of *this* started. My fear creeps in to strangle the hard-fought peace. Mostly, I believe at this point, because I have dwelt on the surface for so long. For long enough. The layer cake needs eating, metabolizing.

My memory jogs to a time when I declined a vocational expansion to prioritize creativity. I bit hard on that and stepped back and wrote like a fiend. I studied, I marveled at what You showed me about Yourself and the power of Your Voice in me.

However, in some quiet corner of my being, a one-sided bargain was struck. I wanted the result of these efforts to rescue me from my responsibilities. This was anathema.

An abomination of Your Purpose. But You allowed me to create by the power of Your Word and You then allowed me to descend deeper into my inner quicksand. The outcome was to be on Your terms. My personal transformation was at stake; Your love for me would not be manipulatively confined or leveraged by my distortions.

Until now, however, and this is the beginning of a new descent, I have harbored disappointment, resentment towards You. Once again, feeling exploited by the One I love; but love is not truly the fuel, it is something else. It is a fraud I am unknowingly perpetrating on myself. You have allowed me to become my own exploiter. How seamless to see my helplessness emerge in this fashion.

Judas, or God to Judas—Your words come back to me in my sleep (when and where I am also *working* on this): *You grip too tightly your emptiness, scraping yields a fraction.* Of course, You are talking to me, and have been, through the words You have given. Especially this now. My bony fingers are tired of clutching, clenching. Your hand waits patiently to receive them into Yours. While I believe You will, my fingers are cemented. Must they be broken?

The symphony begins in the warmth of Your rising Sun. Your creatures cheer me on as my creature rests beside me, reminding me this is the easiest place to be, in Your hands.
Allow me to release.
Soften my grip.
I need this.

August 12

young cub
you have purged
you have cleared
to the nub
now the Essence
of All
you see spilt
in this blood

bones spurned
by Infinity
only Time
can confirm
while your nakedness
your wisdom
beckons my return

walk on
young Lion
be engulfed
by our Tide
so the rolling
of Its Knowing
may restore us
to our Pride

~*Teacher's adieu*

Such a generous coolness, no strain is required to put myself in the way of it. It is here, such kindness.

A friend encouraged this poem, and it takes on fresh meaning. The premise: what if the rich young ruler decides/agrees/chooses to sell everything he owns and follow You? What if he is the one seized in Gethsemane and flees naked as he witnesses the horror unfolding?

What would this have meant for him? If we yield the results of the achievements do we not also agree the achievements themselves are worthless? This is the new insight. Perhaps he was an upstanding human who did loads of good with his efforts and resources—are they all for naught? Or, just the progression of transformation—a rite of passage?

Then the helplessness. How does he walk on? Does he sour on the prospect of his devotion when His Lord is killed? Does He hear of Your resurrection? Do the earthquakes swallow him? Where does he go? Would he have needed to know, or see, or was it already revealed within? Unquestioned. No turning back. There is a starkness of choice. Engulfing surrender.

Today, I see butterflies everywhere I look in the Field, in the Garden. Of course, metamorphosis of souls, or cocoon-womb-tomb. All the same. You sustain me always. As the sparrow flies before me and the breeze picks up ever so slightly, Totem rests more calmly in the coolness. Across millennia, You provide yet another Garden for me to come to, with cedar to smell, and shade for both me and my restful lion hound, as a hummingbird zooms in to view my position. All of this...the breeze out of stillness, the lightness of it. The joy of it. The quenching of it.

You willingly gave it *all*. No one could take it. You risked severing from the One who sustained You, for the Greater, the Greatest Unknown.

How do I not hear You, feel You in this wind out of nowhere? In amazement, I see, as I gather my pack, the Garden's gate, which I close and lock ritualistically, has been blown open. The stone rolls and the Master Gardener comes in for a stroll. And He comforts us with the breeze of Presence on a stifling August morning.

Walk on, young Lion

August 13

As I open the Garden's gate, and then close it with enough force that it latches, I am reminded of the strength of the breeze that opened it wide yesterday.

It is hard not to see meaning in everything here. The breeze that has picked up just now as I have settled down. The hummingbird that caught up with us and followed us here. The butterflies flitting gracefully around us, around my head. The tiger swallowtail, the monarch, the black and blue swallowtail...they are all here. The smell of cedar, of grass. Totem's biscuits on my fingers; it's all here.

I talk with Totem about lying down, calm himself. I tell him *Gentle* when I give him a treat. He sometimes listens while he knowingly looks at me.

We were late again today and Sun was high, which made our arrival at Amen Corner all the sweeter. When I am blinded by Its brightness, I understand more why the crickets and cicadas start to warm up for their morning cantata.

I have been without music for a time. Or, I have avoided it. You gave that back to me here, as I can only sing in response. My childhood best friend, a Wurlitzer upright piano has recently returned home to me. I remember the gift of her at six or seven, around the time I started to stretch beyond my station for the urging. I still have the receipt in the boxes I have sorted. She has borne witness to almost all of it. She was comfort. What tragedy to let the music die, or send her away when I needed her most.

She waited for me to untangle enough threads, to loosen enough to see there was room for her after all and she will now be part of my journey within, as she was before. She knows the way.

The mockingbirds squawk in agreement as a breeze comes from behind. For this muggiest of mornings has caused me to want to leave. It helps to remember the truth that music was with me always. Even when used for the stage shows that were elements of my public life, she was a constant companion, as the Mourning Dove *whoo hoo hoo hoos* from the spire-like cedar before me.

All I hear is music in the Field, in the Garden. Music, piano, and singing are how I carry You into the rest of life. I forget this at my own peril. I rejoice at this awareness. Music, books, my piano—places where I was allowed to *be*. These triumphed over the worldly pressures. They are really the only things I truly treasure, and now, right now, I understand. You are the words, You are the music. Eyes and ears to see and hear, understand and join in Your Beingness. Now writing. My recently recovered boxes of a lifetime of journals indicate that writing, too, has always been with me.

When I remember lengthy seasons of rejection, aloneness, neglect, exploitation by self and other, I can allow myself to go and find the *me* I was with Music with fresh interest and curiosity. I had a family after all, through it all.

You are family of my heart
Respite from the strain

August 14

The newness of what You might be preparing for me is intimidating. Will I be exploited? Will I be consumed? What is this constant holding?

I give as manipulation for control. I give for a fee, for a living, for a vocation. It has given me a *sense* of control. Yet, perhaps on the brink of being given to, I cannot accept without suspicion: is this gift to control me? Therefore, will I lose control, therefore...then what? I dissolve? I die? My worthlessness is exposed?

Garment of salvation, robe of righteousness, this is how You'll clothe me, with the beauty of garments beyond imagining.

A crow sneaks quietly onto the cedar's spire. For the moment, he is silent too. I associate crows with death. What is dying off today that needs consuming? Crow releases a feather and it floats silently. Peaceful descent. No sharp movements. Weightlessness. Landing upon the cedar branch just above my head, it descends, but is held.

Storing up of expectation, for so long, for giving beyond myself. Resentment that travels with me from the tangled blend of feeling no easy option *but* to give. Now, I am expert giver. Time, energy, expertise. It is a trade, it is another bargain struck. It is a commodity. I honestly don't know how I have *done* this for so long. And, I am fairly certain I am hovering about *this* without clarity just yet about what *it* even is.

I quickly come back to breath as I remind myself to inhale and notice the limits of muscle memory to tighten against Life vs. accept the gift of It fully. I believe this is the feast that awaits me. The breeze on this most still of mornings verifies *this*.

The worldly matrix of wisdom is folly. To fling myself into Your outstretched arms...*this* is what I desire and fear simultaneously.

I flick a fluorescent cricket and then remind myself that maybe it's attuning to me today. Maybe I give this place something by being here. This is an agreement I would like to fulfill. By Your Grace, open-handed, *Your covenant with me makes all things ordered and secure.* As I see the first butterfly of the morning, Sun casts Its rays, even through the clouds, and illuminates the page. I am grateful to have waited.

As I depart, it dawns on me...I am a singer. When I sing I must breathe. You fill the openness of the inhale with beautiful vibration from Beyond. The vessel knows this, and I must sing.

August 15
Sunday

Most mornings, I try to predict and rehearse what might be written here.

Today, this quietest of Sundays, the air lies moist and heavy from yesterday's rains, yet it is cooler. I washed Totem's harness and blanket so that he would feel more comfortable.

Unexpected and wary coyote greetings. He or she watched us approach, camouflaged within the perfect den that are the piles of cedar chips dumped where the hay rounds sit. I turn towards Totem; I want to take him another way. He, too, is wary whenever I do this. He may come closer for a treat followed by the click of his leash, but not until he has surveyed around and beyond me to see what chase he might be giving up.

You answer a prayerful wondering with Hawk flying right over me, likely disturbed by our approach, but I am grateful because I haven't seen one in the last couple of days, although the days run together here, and it is sometimes hard to account a true remembering.

The butterflies are active and just as I note the black and blue swallowtail, a tiger swallowtail descends before me from a low branch of Osage Orange onto the rudbeckia. Then three more appear to join in the chase. This must be their time, they love the purple coneflowers.

I wonder if Totem has always known that I would eventually record our times here. I cannot imagine this without him. He was the catalyst. As he approaches 11, I push the foreboding away. We are closer to the end of our time together than our beginning. He weathers wet feet and horsefly bites for me. He is the kindest of fellows.

A coyote on a Thanksgiving Day five years ago ignited my creature-catalyst to his own chase from the front walking trails to this back Field, which I had known existed for decades at that point. For several reasons, it seemed an improbable place to walk together. I hadn't yet considered a harness or treat training to the degree I depend upon them now. The adoring community of this breed might frown upon me for my ways, and yet, Totem and I operate in concert. I trust him to stay with me. It is the exception for him to depart in full primal mode. While those rare occasions occur, I have learned him. He is pack elder now, he stays closer. He guards me as faithfully as ever. When he's ahead of me, he reflexively looks back over his shoulder to check on my status. I say *careful now* to caution him against big movements. He has tutored me into this Being state; I would never have found it without him.

Truly unthinkable, it is our small miracle to have this place and time to walk him this freely. I don't know if he knows how much our daily rhythm gives me my life. His increased neediness has caused me to complain, but I have tried to do away with that for the gift of this. He doesn't need to be thanked. My breath catches to think of life without my watchman.

My three dogs, all Rhodesian Ridgebacks, my cats, and my vocation have filled the dependent child void. Now, Totem is more my peer, or my elderly parent I take for a stroll and feed each day. I wouldn't have it otherwise. My brain was so noisy for so many years; I grew frustrated with him when his movements would interrupt my inner brooding. He has taught me to do differently. He knows no overthinking.

I look at his face only to see some faint whiteness; more truth of his age. I kiss these spots beneath his eyes and shutter away the tears. There is still time. We run together.

The joys we share as we tarry there
None other has ever known

It's the one time that is his
It's the one time that is mine

Come aside by yourselves to a deserted place and rest awhile

Come early and always

August 16

The cardinal welcomes us in song from the crepe myrtle. The traffic hums in the distance as a cricket of another kind. Mondays are a bustling morning. But still, this place holds the quiet. The cedar christens me with droplets of rain it captured for my refreshing. I claim it. It is like oil upon the head.

A flock of nine or ten geese break the silence further. Their announcement: the day has officially begun. The butterflies are still hiding. The mosquitoes are ravenous on this moist morning.

"Fall is almost here. The leaves are turning."

"No they aren't."

"Yes they are. Can't you see it?"

I check my hypothesis against the other Osage Orange and the maple that we pass before we step onto the pink clay and gravel cedar-lined drive. The leaves turn much more slowly than we imagine. The lime-hued hydrangeas lead the way.

I pray hopefully. I try. My reading reminds me that You are like an attentive mother who gives only what is good for the child who never doubts they are loved.

Of course, the father image is easier for me to project onto You. But, this is a gut punch. My mother was mostly attentive when I was sick, and otherwise, quite remote. She was there in body, but her spirit seemed elsewhere much of the time.

To live through this wound, I have manufactured the delusion that I *know* I was loved but *felt* as acutely the disdain of the mother who bore me. So there is no question that I could not see You as a bearer of good things. Perhaps this would have been clearer if I was unwanted. Maybe I was. This, too, is confusing because I was adored at first, or so the story goes.

I think of my Grandmother Joan, whose name I bear, alive for only the first year of my life. Her terminal illness is still a mystery. Apparently, I loved to make her laugh and was constantly in her presence throughout her final year. In my mother's overwhelm with a newborn, a dying mother, and a husband just home from war, it is likely that she left me with Joan quite a lot.

There is a story that Joan hovered over my crib in the middle of the night within 24 hours of her passing. *What was she saying to me?* This served as a sign to her caregivers, my parents, that her departure was close. She was frail enough for my father to carry her to her bed, and then to the hospital. She was alone when she died. And, then, not unlike in my own, the family breakages commenced.

I keep her picture in every room of my home. Every day, she looks straight at me through the photo as she holds my cherubic-infant self in her arms. Sometimes I look back at her, wondering how much she loved me and how I am like her. As I see my mother more and more in my appearance, I am challenged by this reflection of her love thwarted by my own visage.

Prayers sewn into the fibers of your being
Remember your grandmother's embrace?

Was I thinking of her when I wrote these words?

I realize I could skew all of this to an extreme and have spent many therapy hours discussing and dissecting these recollections. I also realize the blame for anything or everything does not solely rest with my mother.

However, a new or dormant connection is how my projection on to You, combined with the faith and hope I have in You, is diminished by the blackness I still carry from this: a mother's disdain versus a loving God who gives good things with maternal affection, comfort, care, joy. My accumulated worthlessness from this wounded root has obscured this possibility completely. Needless to say, You receive father distortions as well. The reading just didn't deliver that particular gut punch today.

But, then, there is my Grandmother Joan who looks at me with Truth in her eyes.

The blue in the sky
Is the blue in my eye
and the wheat, rising, cries
Hallelujah

A crow comes to squawk at my contemplations. He tells me to let it go now. It's an inner death that I can leave here and he will take care of it. Do I believe him?

He squawks his response.

I yield.

Can I?
Really?
Hallelujuh

P.S. This is where my caretaking comes from. I over attend to make up for this lack. I am the loving mother I never had in ways no one really needs, but me.

August 17
Goodbye, Hackberry

Perhaps we are in stunned silence, having lost a friend. A large tree in Field's thicket has fallen from its root. It is not a young tree; it is hard to determine whether it is one of the chosen trees from which the hawks view their emerging prey.

It is a disturbing way to begin a new notebook. I am reeling, processing how many days I have passed that very tree; have I photographed it? With or without its leaves? It is not until we arrive at Amen Corner that I can see the void in the thicket it has left in its wake. A Carolina wren joins me as we bear tribute to the enormous loss.

Who will see it before it is chopped up into pieces? How to memorialize? Who even cares?

The metaphors are inescapable. Of course, that tree is as old as any life that is considered long by human standards, maybe less. We fall to the ground and are bid adieu by rites and rituals that assist in our body's return to the earth, while our souls depart for the hereafter. Who will care? Who will remember? Why does it matter?

My aging sentinel paws at me as if on cue. I think he wants a kiss because he senses my anguish, but what he really wants is a treat. He wants me to bribe him to stay put a little longer. That quickly I am returned to the stuff of life.

Yesterday I reviewed some photos from this long season I am still passing through. It is hard to describe the emptiness I see. Attempts at being myself—but, sadly, all that comes across to me is the heaviness behind my eyes and I am grateful I didn't force myself through it and *try* to become something I am not. *All I hear is the Carolina wren's high-trilling warble in agreement.*

I wonder if the fallen tree is part of my coming to my senses here. Did it hold fast until I did? This is my hope: to make meaning of its witness to my metamorphosis. From its branches did the Hawk pray for me? Did it request that I could see life through another lens—*Hawk's view?*

Thank You for the tree
that saw me
and stayed with me

if I fall alone
may You carry me Home
may my Life matter
for the Greater

if no one sees
may Your Love stand in my absence
may my uprooting be the vehicle
for that Love to come and hold my space
by Your Loving Purpose, Fullness and Grace

Amen and Amen, says the Carolina wren.

August 18

I stoke my losses with shame.
So much so that the flame does irreparable harm if I get too close.

I can never grieve what is mine to grieve if it all comes down to my failure, my responsibility.

I am the most dense creature in this Field. The hackberry's corpse remains. Your Golden Orb shines directly upon its fallen limbs, so, You know.

There is an ominous spread of fur on the gravel drive. I wonder who else fell to the ground overnight. You must know.

It is rare to encounter so much overt death here in just these couple of days; yet, I know it is a constant. As it is in the world. How do You stay current with all of this loss?

I have secreted mine away behind the stealthy invisibility cloak of therapist and client, and writer of stories about You. Perhaps all have been worthy attempts, but I have not had the kind of clearance I do presently to slowly unfurl my own losses fully. There is nothing holding me back and *buried deep resides yearning for a life liberated.*

17 years ago, dad, you collapsed due to a heart event. I remember the two times I saw you just previous to your short hospital stay, which rendered you incommunicative and on life support. Lost to me. I prognosticate that you knew what had happened at the onset two days earlier, but that you didn't let on because you wanted to go, which leaves me to imagine that mom let you languish. She was your partner in this.

I'm sorry were your last conscious words to my mother. For what? For leaving? For knowing you were leaving, having played a role in it? For wanting to leave? For all that came before?

Any time I extracted myself there was some sort of magnetic pull, from me, or from you, or from both of us, back to each other. A fused, blended mess. *A black swallowtail enters and I wonder if it's you, or death.*

I have clearly not recovered. I hate that my mother's sentiment, meant to disempower or shame me, or so it feels, is ultimately true: "I don't think you have ever grieved your father." No, I have been too busy gorging on helpings of failure and shame. I am *so all-powerful*, that all of these items have to do with me, and what I have or haven't done right or wrong. To escape this vortex, I medicate with overwork, exhaustion, bitterness, and resentment.

Totem kisses my salty tears as I witness a caterpillar tenuously climbing its silk, and I wonder, *will I survive this passage?* The tether is so delicate and I have let this infected wound reside in me for so long. 17 years, 20 years, 27 years, all of my life. Because it seems there is not enough of You to care for all of it. Except, the sparrows, the hackberry, the just-fallen creature in the Field tell me otherwise.

Fear stalks me in my sleep. This may mean things are shifting in my waking hours; I'd like to hope this is true. I think of a recent picture of my mother, my niece, my nephew. I feel an urge to run to my mother's bedside and receive her smile and tell her it is okay. I mourn what never was and what never will be simultaneously, even if now more approachable. If I am to go, You will need to make the way plain. I do not want to move out in front of Your guiding Hand as I am prone to do. While there are hesitations, I do not want to postpone.

The finches feed on the fruit and the berries of the cedar. They are putting on a show, drawing my attention back to Your minute care. The sprinklers come on to signal their closing act. The play here will continue indefinitely, while, for now, the water quenches and softens.

I will try to recover a life after losing you
but I will never forget

I might try *less* so that I might actually recover. Forgetting is impossible. The wreckage is piled high; there is no getting around it, except to live it all through.

August 19

We shortcut a bit today. It has rained and it is humid and buggy, a typical mid-August morning. Yet the Field holds true to its beauty as the birds begin to sing.

The hero theme continues to reveal itself. How *it* is what I am gripping, among other things, and I consider that I grip this emptiness because it is all I have left of you, dad. Possible. Probable.

At my age, your cracks were not only showing, but also gaping. I do the math and wonder how the hand-me-down-hero role was devouring you, how you were medicating. To *do* better, I have tried to remain conscious to prevent the complete destruction of my life. It goes without saying that You sustained me through these years of desperate flailing.

I take in how the clouds are moving towards us from the Field's edge where I accessed my initial helplessness during the recent years of this inner wilderness wandering. I can see myself walking and screaming at You, beating the air with complaints, agitation, resentment, bitterness. You gave me this Field while You waited for me to empty all of that poison. Now I grip the emptiness because fullness is a mystery. While I know I live it; it just doesn't compute. Abiding is a kind of *un*thinking, after all. But the blended cocktail of confusion, loneliness, anger, insecurity, seems bottomless and constant.

I hear Sally's familiar baying. She is also constant. Totem is constant. The ground beneath me is constant. There is more constant in You than in this regime that loves to shackle me to the pittance of what the world might offer me as consolation—and that it is, a momentary consolation.

I shift my gaze to the cedar treetops that line the gravel drive from a different Garden vantage point. Cedars of Lebanon, donned with anointing rains, once again collected for my passing baptism.

What else is there?
Take it from me
Help me release it fully
Wash and renew my mind

It dawns on me that I prefer to write in the Garden. The Field is for emptying, the Garden is for fullness. Pay attention.

Last night I dreamed a dream. It was a morning dream, really. A little girl turned to me and said, *if you ask from your heart, you can have anything.*

Reading this morning. Your Words level me daily.

Whoever does not doubt in his heart, but believes that those things he says will be done, he will have whatever he says.

Thank You.

August 20

This entire time, I have neglected to put my feet in the grass, boots off, to feel the earth beneath me.

Mourning dove, cicada, Carolina wren greet me even in this late Summer rain. Once again, we are a feast for the mosquitoes, while a skunk sighting keeps us from our normal turns around the Field. It is always quieter on rainy days. I never mind.

When I reread my words, I can see the day-to-day movements. This surprises and helps. The rain picks up and I am not sure if my Witness Tree's canopy will hold. In a breath, or two, the shower lightens, and then increases.

As we are pushed out of the Garden, the gate into the graveyard is fortuitously open. We can conclude our time under the maple that is Hawk's most frequent perch. Totem considers scaling the fence that encloses us to chase a squirrel, and then thinks better of it. The towering maple shelters a stone bench which affords us a few more hidden moments between showers.

I go to therapy today. I will talk about you, once again, dad, and being consumed, exploited, and the vestiges of toxicity I am trying to release, or, better, asking to be healed.

I note this because tomorrow is the anniversary of your passing, and my intention is to visit another graveyard nearby, for, somehow, while everyone else has departed the area, you are still here. Whatever remains of you.

My plan is to bring the hackberry's leaves from this Field and leave them with you to honor your departure. I can see the uprooted elder from my graveyard bench. If I am the seedling, the offshoot, I am ready to flourish even if I need one more winter to deepen my roots in the good soil You have provided.

Unbound by time or timing, You can grow me into the gap, a sound tree that retains my connection to him, but I believe it is time to fill out.

How Your breeze comes when it does and breaks the heaviness. The souls here know this is always Your Grace.

Inhale, *better.*

Exhale.

Listen for the robin and the baby birds. Take this with me. It is sustenance, it is Communion, it is Bread of Life.

August 21
Anniversary

It is a rare occurrence to be housebound by rain. A Saturday morning confinement. Yet, it is an important day. I thought I would make it to your gravesite. But, I think it is not meant to be.

Instead, Totem is covered up under warm laundry. A palliative. The cats gingerly find their places next to him. They refuse to be left out.

The Garden has become an unanticipated gift for my imagination to recapture itself. I will practice that more.

Also unanticipated: inner quiet and contentment. No need to compulsively process your passing, dad. That's part of releasing the captive from her heroic machinations to just *be* today. In fact, I think that would be a great kindness.

The piano you gave me is here. I think I will go be with my friend and play and sing for us.

August 22

The bugs are voracious this tropical Southern morning. We yearn for our Garden respite. Somehow there is always a breeze under Osage Orange's arms.

A shower threatens and Totem stands guard and I wonder how to sit comfortably with my feet on the earth while I write.

I feel an eagerness and clarity which I have hoped for, longed for, and prayed for. My notes and scribbles tell me more. And I feel gratitude for Your continued healing of me which You have kindly undertaken.

Aliens and strangers, no continuing city—the Home within. Where the Beyond lives. No veil of separation. That has been removed. *Bring a clean vessel to the House of the Lord.* But I cannot clean it nor bring it. Without You none of this is possible.

It is challenging to keep the wondering of the times at bay because they seem like no other. Troubling, devastating desolation heightens and sharpens all of it. *We walk the knife's blade*—but there is scant conversation, minimal community, everyone is grappling. There is only relief to consider the Truth of Your movements throughout and within. I am not held captive.

The rabbi places his head in his hands in utter sickness of soul. He wails: *What opportunities have we missed? Who have we passed by on the side of the road? Who have we surrendered to waywardness by our passivity? Blindness? Denial?*

Wickedness seems to have no bounds. For Your continual guidance and direction we are beyond need. We are desperate.

Thank You for the wren's song that joyously interrupts this turmoil. Thank You for the delight of this Garden that brings me back to the Truth of this unsullied moment. I know You pass through here with me. I know we are not alone. *The joys we share as we tarry there, none other has ever known.*

But may others know.

August 23

The fog is dense, visibility is poor. Totem just barked at a passerby. He is protector. I can hear geese in the far background. We are all just trying to live through whatever this time holds. I am hopeful there will not be an end to this practice. But there could be. I must flex with the demands of the time. There is little that is *constant* except change.

I am Jacob. *Constantly* allowing my fear and scarcity mindset to dictate how I hedge and act on my own for survival. The reptile brain flourishes in this leanness. *Isn't it best to prepare for catastrophe?* Rumors of war. Deaths in our community. Unbearable truths. The moisture hangs in the air and we can only see so far in front of us. We are as fragile as the spider attempting to build its web. The flimsy stakes so delicate. The mosquitoes feast on our blood.

Jacob was creative. He anticipates, he spent, he drew drama unto himself. His first love was thwarted. He betrayed, he was betrayed, he fled. He desired everything You had for him, yet fought it all the while. Seeking his father's blessing. Stealing it even. Avoiding his brother until he had to pass through his land and face him down.

You never said *God of Abraham* or *Isaac*, but *God of Jacob*. This is why I was curious. Also, the mystery of the Man who wrestled him aside the river. Was it a dream? Apparition? A version of himself? Angel? Brother? You? All are possible. First recording of a physical encounter with the Supernatural. The story holds for millennia—there is power in this.

Jacob is midlife-ing in his crisis. He is tired of carrying the burdens for his families, his parents, his uncle. He is weary of holding all of the weight and responsibilities. Yet, in his own way, he continues to add to them *constantly*. He is pack mule and plow horse.

He does the unthinkable in his state of panic. A most fatal error: he sends his family ahead with his gift offerings to his disgruntled twin whom he is certain still holds the stolen-birthright grudge.

I am Esau. Unrecognized hero. Angry that the eldest is often passed over. It is a raw deal. *I stick in the craw of my parents to punish them for their lapse, my hubris.* There is no return, there never will be. The hero never wins. *I bear the brunt of my parents' needs in Jacob's absence, so I medicate with wine, killing, conquering, marrying, concubines.* It never satisfies, and it never will.

The injury renders me ever needy. My limp, a <u>constant</u> reminder.

At midlife, I sacrificed my own family. It has never been the same and never will be, unless somewhere behind this murky veil You have another path for me. Totem, too, tries to see past and into the fog. With Your Sun rising, we expect to see more clearly. Help us, help us. Guide our path. Be our eye.

You are Mine
You are loved
You are not forgotten

You are the same—unchanging, everlasting in lovingkindness.
You bear us up
The waters will not overtake

We have a holy calling
according to Your Purpose
and grace given to us in Christ Jesus
before time began

Fear not
Nothing can separate us from Your love

In Your Book, my days were fashioned—
All of them

August 24

I look over my shoulder and the black swallowtail honors my gaze. And then the chickadee sings. Totem clears a mosquito by chomping the air.

Yesterday, I wrote about Jacob and Esau. Last night, You place my own brother's handwriting in front of me just after reading from the very book he gave my father for Christmas over 40 years ago. *40 years in the wilderness, wandering.*

It will take me some time to digest this. But my own inner father wants to reach out immediately. Maybe I will. I am also the prodigal son who has abandoned the family and is perhaps *coming to my senses.* Love abounds. *I don't have to live like this.*

Yet I have held much judgment. We have all lost much. Even if a necessary hiatus, I am convicted of my self-righteousness, the inevitable result of the caretaking-hero's path. I felt exploited and consumed with nothing left to offer anyone—yet continued a vocation with responsibilities, which I allow to squeeze any remaining life force out of me. This became another excuse to avoid a great deal. No wonder *Reckoning* didn't go where *I* thought it should. It was pure, but I tainted it. In my failure, my eyes were open, but my heart was not. It came by grace for *me* to see *me.*

I sense you are guiding me to loosen even more of my grip, the arbitrary stranglehold around those things I see as obstacles. I will try with Your help. Please show me. Please guide me.

I pray for a reunification within and without. For Your resources to *do* these things. Forgive my waywardness.

Thank You for showing me the way.

August 25

Just as I think I have swindled myself out of the full Field experience, sirens from the town trigger the family of coyotes to howl their morning cantata in perfect pitch. I am reminded of the hidden risks that lie in wait along Field's borders. This protected spot is a treasure. The wren joins in on cue in agreement.

Of course, a morning following a day of richness would be the morning I feel a funky doubt creep in. It is likely the youngest me protesting that she feels too exposed. My reading is too poignant to miss Your direction, however. I remind myself of this.

I search for my brother and find pictures of him. He is older, but still him, and my soul lurches to my throat in joy and sorrow simultaneously. My unworth crowds out the possibility that he would benefit from having a sister in his life. This is like a crowbar to my inner root ensconced in the hard-packed clay of fear and shame. But You want this bed plowed. There is no more avoiding.

Of course, it is close to the anniversary of my father's passing and likely the day of, or day before his funeral 17 years ago.

I recall being with my brother at your bedside, dad. He wanted me with him:

He secures your resting place. This is a great help. Except I can't breathe and feel the weight of everything else closing in. The loss of everything...perhaps necessary, but I did not know it then. It is the second time you leave me like this. Or, did I orchestrate that all along?

Remember, remember your young you buried underneath. She couldn't even process this departure. *Once you left your body, I left the room. What was the point of remaining? How were those last arduous breaths? Were you afraid? How could you not have been terrified? I am so sorry I couldn't do anything. Death too strong. It stole you from me, from us all.* As the hackberry has fallen, you left a gaping black hole, immediately felt, spinning and dark, waiting for me.

I hope you heard us singing you home. I hope you heard me singing 'You are my Sunshine...'. I hope there was no pain and a smooth passage. It is unimaginable.

How do I go from here? The geese fly in formation overhead, announcing their arrival. This is a reminder that I am not alone and cannot go on as I have, in exile. It is past time to let others in. Please help me. I already sense Your help.

I feel the need to reach out. Show me, don't let me miss it. I am listening better now that my tears have softened the clay in my ears.

Look to the rock from which you were hewn and to the hole of the pit from which you were dug.

...you were thrown out into the open Field, where you yourself were loathed on the day you were born. And when I passed by you and saw you struggling in your own blood, I said to you—LIVE

miry clay

August 27

I fill Totem's bowl to the brim, for he is thirsty. I leave a sip for myself. As it should be.

The Garden is enclosed on all sides by a tightly-picketed white fence, which seems to quiet things. It is a noisy morning. Totem decided to run off first thing. He looked over his shoulder at me in glee for having done so. As it should be.

I fidget to find a way for my feet to touch the earth under Osage Orange, for I know the sacred connection will hold me throughout this day.

We recount elements of our story over dinner. I am the more forgetful one. He loves to share his memory of the Buddhist nun's traveling gaze fixed upon me while sitting outside of the chapel. He interprets that she sees love in our shared humanity. I interpret the silent encounter as a reprise of the Beautiful Gate: *I am the lame man, she is Peter and John. She identifies my faith, paralyzed by my own fusion of self with worldly pursuits, blended with elements of the heroic delusion which ravage and render me immobile.* I was always losing ground, even while rising to the challenge and carrying ever more responsibility. No inner comfort, only the strain of stretching. It was what it was. The soil within was more hard-packed then. It had just begun to soften.

Totem settles and I wonder where the hawks are, and the lapis bluebird, a rare variety from South America. I wonder if the heat became too much for them and they moved north for some coolness. Their songs greet me most mornings. As I write, I think I hear their very song from tucked away in the Garden's arborvitae. This longing for Your creatures is almost always received and answered. Even if it's the mockingbird's repetitive songs. She attempts to fill the void.

This week has brought much plowing. Another pastor dies close to your anniversary, dad. Another tragic loss. I think again of my brother and what You want me to do. Don't allow me to postpone or distract. A woodpecker types above me, confirming You hear me.

Thank You.

His compassions fail not
They are new every morning
Great is Your faithfulness

What do you mean, Sleeper?
Arise!

Your ears shall hear a word behind you
Saying, 'this is the way, walk in it'
whenever you turn to the right hand
or whenever you turn to the left

August 28

There will be a funeral today for a person I have known throughout various seasons. A tragic, sudden loss. He was one year younger than myself—almost two.

This is what I came to face. How many days do I consider myself impervious? Immune? *Pride of life.*

Totem lies down—I have such a companion with me. We brave the humidity and mosquitoes together. He smells the air, he lingers, gratefully. I face inward. Garden's interior space pulls me today.

There is much to *do* always, and my exhaustion is still a reality. I sense You do not need me working. You are working in and through my *weakness*. Always, always when I am not aware. Grace upon grace. Like Totem's calmness beside me.

The healing happens outside the gate. Your travail for us was outside the gate, where we are to find You. My ransom was paid outside the gate. The coyotes sing together with the sirens. Amen Corner, Coyote Corner. The woodchip piles are their dens, I'm sure. I am not afraid, but there are many of them. A pack, a family, a tribe.

The healing happens outside the gate. The lame man goes into the temple with his first steps. Going to temple did not heal him. Going to church did not heal me. The Temple is an inner reality as the Field and this Garden are now within me. There is plenty to find—and there is always beauty with the healing, and then, the wholeness.

He suffered outside the gate
I must go out to Him

August 29
Sunday

The sprinklers are on.

This means I missed Garden's Act One and the finches have already departed, having taken their bows. I hear a bluebird's song, but not the one I am looking for—the lapis-blue variety. Overnight it seems the crookneck squash have formed and matured.

In this moment of *exhale* I wonder if these entries will mean anything to anyone. Knowing full well that now that I anticipate their recording with joy. That *should* be enough. I think it is now.

These past few days hold fatigue mixed with an unspooling. Perhaps the inner ground is turned over and awaits its Fall planting. When I read these pages, I can see their ebb and flow. Your stream of current within me now finds its expression, by Your power and Your grace.

I shift my posture because a noisy troupe of crows are corralling themselves. Hawk must be close by. Even above me in Osage Orange. For several days, I have missed the hawks. Their preferred spots must be changing as Your Golden Orb climbs higher, later. Fall approaches even with this tropical heat and moisture. I think I hear the lapis bluebird's song mixed in to the fray. I scan the Garden for them, although I usually spot them in the Field's bordering thicket between Amen and Coyote Corners, their favorite place to forage. The crows arrive from all directions and I wait for Hawk to show itself. However, without warning, the troupe moves on—their cries more distant now.

It is Sunday, the quietest of mornings, as I always say. Unhurried. I consider the loose ends, the want for continued clarity. The ways I pile on expectation upon creation and how I must yield while also not sabotaging. I start too many books, and I often start reading them from their middle. When I find a sweet spot in my own *work*, my unworthiness causes me to forget. She feels exposed without her crown and cape and frantically searches for the next thing to *do*, to *please*. More and more hollow this artifice becomes. I must support her *better*.

The birdsong in the spired cedar causes me to shift again because it sounds exactly like the lapis-blue. Is a mockingbird pulling my leg? I hear voices, too, but I think we are shielded enough from view. Totem fidgets and the crows can't seem to organize themselves. The distracting noisiness continues. Your Sun rises enough to blind me and illuminate the passing shadows of the crows.

You are faithful to complete. My prayer: that You are strong for me in these, my weaknesses. Perhaps the good soil is airing out and needs further amendment by the Master Gardener.

August 30

I cannot stop my agitation this morning. When others come to *our* Field on *my* timeline, it rankles me more than anything because it is challenging to walk Totem anywhere. I feel as if this should be self-evident to anyone within range. When we arrive at the Field, I expect it to be empty.

A brown and white gull with huge V-shaped flapping wings flies over for the second day in a row. I have not been able to classify it yet.

I feel protective of my rhythms. This is always a sacred window. Others cycle in and out, and this can be exhausting. My circle is needfully small. While I do not need a lot of contact, I do not need to be monastic either. Somewhere in between. I am too sensitive to the agitation of others. And all are fairly agitated right now, myself included.

As I read these entries I see Your handiwork; I will continue to record as a way of seeing. Please also continue to soften my inner ground. I have paused reaching out to my family. I am unsure but am fairly clear that it was for me to feel the weight of all that I have been *heroically* dragging along with me, and then to prayerfully release with Your assistance.

I understand the woodpecker's tap-tap-tapping as confirmation. That may be my own projected distortion. While this does not feel like a helpful write, the *order* of things has been reversed—I will walk it out now.

Reading Your Word immediately calms.
Perfect love casts out fear
Fear involves torment
Love casts out torment

Onward to the Field we go, young lion.

SEPTEMBER

September 1

There is not much more glorious than this sacred ground after a drenching rain supplants the heat and allows room for cooler breezes. The cicadas are quiet because it is not warm enough for them to vibrate.

When I imagine what the Beautiful Gate opens into, I have only imagined something slightly better than whatever came before. A gateway to more wilderness wandering—like Christian in Pilgrim's Progress. While that still could be true, I now consider that a Garden, which requires a devoted tending to yield fruit, is likely on the other side of the gate, as this one. How many days have I passed it by and not thought to enter through the gate and experience the Garden like this? Years. Too busy with my own thoughts and beliefs about what was real.

All the while, You have been silently welcoming and inviting me. But I was too busy believing that this Field was all that was. Even if that was partly true, and that the Field is where the Treasure lies, what is the Field's value? It is good soil for planting the Garden; it is fertile ground for fruitfulness. The finches chirp their validation and the breeze seconds their motion.

I am astonished by these insights. Simple. Profound. Before my very eyes, for years, yet, I have not entered in, nor abided. I have been too busy gasping for air. The stranglehold of my default programming, which I allowed to consume me while I mistakenly called it love, family, ministry, service, friendship. These distortions are all being challenged now. Again, the crystal clear birdsong validates.

Thank You for this revelation. I am desperate for it.

September 3

The sainted coolness of Fall has arrived early. The world is aflutter with gratitude. The wet lingers and chills, so my time with Totem is limited in this spot. Moisture everywhere and he is not a water dog, but he is ever the good sport.

Hawk flies overhead as we begin our Field trek. Our secret language—You have heard my yearning as I have missed You. The siren coyote song is activated more and more each morning. It is clear there is a pack, and the mowers begin their droning too early.

It is Friday. September's first Friday, and our wedding anniversary. Everything since that beautiful day has changed. We are both joyful and appreciative for our endurance. Not ours, actually, but the binding agent of You. Nothing could be further from rhetoric. It is all we know and all we have.

I have sky-screamed at You many a morning here. *What are You doing? Why this suffering?* At least for now, I feel the peace in the Garden that is on the other side of, or adjacent to, that travail. There is fullness, joy, but also an accompanying sorrow for others lost or losing loved ones and life itself. It is hard to believe in Your Love when this affliction transpires. You are in control, but have given time and place and power to this darkness that now abounds. You carry me. You receive Your children of this life for the next despite the consuming blindness. How can we not stumble? Not to speak of the collateral damage from our fall.

I look up to the cedar spire and a blonde-headed Red-tailed Hawk has graced our presence. It has come to watch the show from on high. The troupe of blue jays clucks their signals—they are on high alert. Hawk is undeterred. The robins sound their distress calls to their young to take cover and stay hidden.

What a gift on this day. I have never been so close and shared this stillness with such a beauty. Its blonde head is curious. A female? A youth? Some finches float in and then realize...in one blink, it is gone. I believe it is still nearby, hunting its fruit.

What does this mean? You see me. You know me. You cover me with Your wings. You wish for me to look through Your lens and see the Higher Hawk's view.

What a gift. Completely unexpected. Bookending this beautiful day as You always do. No matter where we are, You are here. Even when not seen.

the root of bitterness defiles
unleavened bread of sincerity and truth

let a man examine himself
let him eat of that bread and drink of that cup

the simplicity of Christ we are corrupted from

Stand
Gird waist in *truth*
Breastplate of *righteousness*
Shod feet with *preparation* of gospel of peace
Above all shield of faith, *faith through Jesus' Name*
Helmet of salvation ~ *spiritual mind of wholeness, protects against the fracturing of thinking alone*

September 4

Sit still, daughter
I forgot Totem's water, but we are quenched in other ways on this moist, dew-filled morning.

Sit still, daughter
When the family of deer appear, they look startled by our presence, more cautious than usual, potentially threatened.

Sit still, daughter
When my restlessness or eagerness serves up constant distraction, I leave loose ends hanging only to beat myself up with them.

Sit still, daughter
Not acting hastily as You stitch the threads together, desiring my relying, abiding. Through passive activity, I be and believe. I see Martha in the kitchen—urging Mary from her good part. Responsibility, action, performance, doing...

Sit still, daughter
Even in this, this moving meditation I require myself to *do*. I must write, of course.

Sit still, daughter
So, I put my pen aside.

Sit still, daughter
   in rest and return you shall be saved
   in quiet and confidence shall be your strength

September 5
Sunday

The sweetness of Sunday morning Silence in this sanctuary. We await the rains but Your golden light still shines through.

Soul stirring, last night truly activated—more like a soul sickness. The stake in the ground against or beyond the temporal. My focus wavers—I am so distracted by the unnecessary. Focused in on fear of *not having enough*. Clutching to the life I am meant to lose this way. Be fed by Bread, Water, Blood, Vine, all of it that You are.

The disciples row and row in the chop for three or four miles. Effort, exhaustion. You appear and get them to safe harbor immediately. Those few miles can look like an eternity. Three-quarters of a life even. But then You come in with swiftness and power.

The Cooper's hawk has shown itself today, hunting in another Osage Orange, framed by the second-story portico nearby. Your breezes continue to blow Your Spirit confirmation.

I want to enjoy the fruits of this Life without longing for my former imprisonment. There is a fine line. Help me not to stumble here.

Please crystallize, consolidate *Your message* in me, I want its confounding simplicity. Even in my busy mind, I think I can process what is so clearly Beyond. Your Mind, Your Thoughts through me. I sense You are always communicating with me in ways that I miss because my perception is too small. I desire to be obedient. Truly. I cannot without You.

As Totem falls asleep next to me, I thank You for this glorious Communion.

September 6
Labor Day

The dew drenches. The mist blankets. The deer pass like hulking shadows just ahead of us, reminding me *As the deer panteth for the water so my soul longeth after Thee. You alone are my heart's desire and I long to worship Thee. You alone are my strength my shield, to You alone may my spirit yield. You alone are my heart's desire and I long to worship Thee.*

My heroic, pained child surfaces in the crisis state of things. I consume information and I pay a hefty price. I feel the pressure. I feel responsible. I feel a failure. I have no idea what to do.

You tell me through Your Word to return and rest, in quiet. I realize by consuming worldly wisdom, I am bereft of that Center and feel the abyss of fear open wide inside of me. The predictions of catastrophe corrupt my inner peace. I do not want to be ignorant, but do not want to fall prey to giving more power away to fear.

During a recent season, I yearned for time, more time. Yet, when I receive the gift, I flail. It is hard to find a rhythm and then to stick to it. The diligence and discipline I lack unless it is about being needed.

You have so clearly carried us. You care for those who have nothing. You want us to surrender whatever we clutch—open hands. You flourish me with your loving-kindess, guiding my focus all the while.

How long will the hackberry lie there?

I feel convicted about many, many things. Agreeing to be caught by the baited hooks of worldly designs. Allowing my *want*, my *lack*, my lusts to dominate. Only by Your Grace did we make it through. You continue to hold us up. You have granted our healing, to become more whole, and hopefully, more useful. I do not want to ruminate towards scarcity and scramble to figure *it* out. Please confirm the work of my hands. Give me the strength to row with my back to the goal—even in the stormy chop. If You are all I have, that is everything. Allow my light to shine brightly for You.

The futility of my mind acts up. It wants to think through, it *thinks* it can. The only thing that is True is Jesus. The Mourning Dove *whoo hoo hoo hoos* in agreement.

Just a few short days ago my mind was quiet, but, again, caught by the bait of decimation and death. Yet, You care endlessly. Again, my hero child feels so responsible for all she cannot possibly handle. Please help me with this. In Jesus' Name.

The dove sings its lullaby above my head, slow and steady as it tries to comfort me.

I lift up my soul.

Whatever you ask in my Name, that I will do
Abide
Your Word always confirms.

Cause me to know the way in which I should walk
for I lift up my soul to You

September 8
Totem's 11th Birthday

The mist blanket is so thick, we cannot tell until we are all the way in that the Field has been mowed entirely. Even Amen Corner, which had been preserved as a pasture all Summer. Its high grasses bordered the clearly mowed path along Field's crest. Each morning, I look back over my shoulder to see the golden hues Your Orb casts upon the waves of grass bending by Your breezes. From Amen Corner it is something to behold. Your beauty is impossible to describe.

Your Name—the Name. Third John capitalizes Name. The Beautiful Gate; the healing of Your Name. I keep listening for Your Name. The silence is deafening. Our souls have starved for it for far too long. We have forgotten to remember the only Name worth remembering.

We encounter a coyote on the hunt. I can see it stalking something in the mist, not unlike my quest for You this morning. I am grateful for the crows' cawing—they sound the alarm. I retreat to the Garden—at some point the coyote catches our scent and alerts the pack. Its shrieks and howls startle Totem and I am also grateful to be in close proximity to the Garden's enclosure. The sprinklers turn on and startle us. The survival exhilaration is in sharp contrast to the soul sickness of my lack. I am quickly made aware of this and am, in a way, relieved. The threat of the coyote's stalking is real—my system responds accordingly, and I immediately flee, with vigilant urgency, to safety before the stress immediately retreats.

The heavy pall of scarcity is not able to coexist with this primal instinct. Rather, it is an inner deadness in need of Your refreshing. I inhale the breeze of revelation.

My soul's sickness, the fear of *never enough*—scraping, clutching yielding a fraction—is a haunting signal, like the crows letting me know my inner exiled daughter needs some more digging out. This simple acknowledgement eases it. Aggressive casting out is not the prescription. You want me to attend, and then tend within, like this Garden. Till the soil, plant the seed; care for my inner Field and Garden. Join with Your goodness, the Holy Root.

I missed this time yesterday. I supplemented in other ways. It was a good day in its own right, but not like the day when I breathe Your breezes and sense Your Spirit embodying my torso. Perhaps the *lack* is that lack of Spirit. I am digging her *me* out of quicksand, so I must continue with vigor. Thank You for showing me. I need Your help.

My mind is busy both morning and evening and I know better than to let this stand. Lovingkindness in the morning, faithfulness in the evening. Declare the day.

I am poor and needy; yet the Lord <u>thinks</u> upon me

I know the thoughts that I think toward you, thoughts of peace and not of evil

What is highly esteemed among men is an abomination to God

If the root is holy, so are the branches

Deepen the root.
Thank You, thank You for this Treasure.
It is Bread, It sustains, It satisfies.

September 9

Sun's light and rise time is changing. Totem is taken by the new smells unleashed by the rows of mowed brush. Surely the coyotes and deer have made their mark by now. We have arrived past their time.

As the realities of our world continue to churn, I am reminded, as he sits next to me, why, and for whom I have found this haven of rest. Totem, my most anxious and needy of Ridgebacks would not settle until his demand was met. A place for him to stretch his legs fully, to see and smell everything. He was unbearable without it, and at 11 now, if we miss a day, our secret language is conveyed by our mutual restlessness. He compromises and slows for me. He sits with me willingly. I kiss him 11 times as he listens to me read, as I am conscious of the preciousness of this shared space. When viewing pictures of his littermates, I am shocked by how young he looks in comparison. Yet, we are in the final season. Perhaps together.

Both males, now including my cat, are my soul's mates. I dare not consider a different life. I must inhale their presence and fix their image upon my Being, for they are Life in this life, they are Lifeblood, and Love in its fullness. What a grace to have them as gifts their love keeps opening to me. To You I am grateful that You knew I needed their steadiness.

Your Sun shines through the front portico on Its new path, a slower Autumnal trajectory. You ignite spots in my eyes that I must look around in order to see Hawk's belly mirroring Your rays. But I know that I need their penetrating vibration and frequency to inhabit my cells and be light for the windows to my soul.

Bruno is leaving to meet family and clear effects—not an easy journey. Yet, his approach is buffeted by his wholeness. With his leaving today, even for a short time, I am pained. Not grasping for solitude. There is no one I would rather spend time with. For this too I am grateful, this refreshing.

While I must move on for the day, I request Your courage. An unshirking courage, unflinching in the face of what is being revealed. Amen.

I am the Lord Your God. Open your mouth wide and I will fill it.

Why do you spend money for what is not bread and wages for what does not satisfy? Listen carefully to Me. Eat what is good and let your soul delight itself in abundance.

I am the bread of life. He who comes to Me shall never hunger, and he who believes in Me shall never thirst.

He shall deliver you in six troubles, yet in seven; no evil shall touch you.

September 10

Twenty years ago today, my family traveled to New York for my Grandmother's funeral. The next fateful day would usher in an unspeakable nightmare. Save us, Lord.

Joshua: do not look at the giants on either side of you, look straight ahead, only as far as your next step. Stay focused on Me. My focus is too easily distracted lately. I feel weary; still allowing the inner hero to veer off and look for the catastrophe for which she is somehow responsible. For far too long this has been her currency of worth and value.

I am so grateful for Your lovingkindness. Prayer, praise, and song prohibit thought. They overtake thought, their vibration consumes toxin.

More rumors of war abound in earnest. The plot thickens. I stare into the apocalyptic abyss. I fail the test to row with my back to it. *Be my strength my shield.* Wow, this. is. it...*to You alone may my spirit yield.*

The hum of life drowns out the birds. The crickets are quiet. Not enough heat. Fall arrives. The arugula sprouts through the soil. I feel the need to receive Your Word—Food, Bread, Water. Thank you mockingbird, for your perpetual repertoire. Thank you, Totem, for being with me.

above all
through all
in all

that they all may be one. As You, Father are in Me and I in You, that they also may be one in Us, that the world may believe that You sent Me

those that wait on the Lord shall renew their strength

when you are weak, then I am strong

September 11

The mockingbird meets me with her usual myriad of motifs, masquerading as anyone but herself. Sonic camouflage. The wren is Morse-coding from the southeast fence.

Fidelity. Or, lack thereof. This generational curse upon my father's line. The men betray themselves as they betray everyone else. Then, they are betrayed. By disease, by resentment, by death, by others, while the rest of us are collaterally damaged.

I was likely born into infidelity. Grandmother Joan looks at me lovingly but sternly through the picture—*don't you dare not live your destiny! They have lived their life—you live yours!*

Yet, I betray myself by searching for crisis. I have bound myself to this captor in every way. Even now, my thoughts drift to my current preoccupations, a roving list of online forage to choose from, all of which morphs into a runaway train. All of it is tasty bait.

How now? Deprivation, clutching, controlling, doubting. Too familiar with this state of being. Except it is anti-being. The hero disguises my own demise, or soul killing.

I cannot see, or have not seen how all of this connects. Like the birds singing now, or even *just* the mockingbird, I am flitting from thing to thing. Not landing, staying confused, waiting for the crisis to clarify. Colluding in its manifestation.

My marriage birthed into the context of my father's infidelity. My young adulthood swindled by his waywardness. The miscarriage, the miscarriage of an unborn life. I would have completely evaporated in more parenting. Betrayal from all corners. It's like a hall of mirrors.

Fidelity to Your Life in me—hewing so closely, this ingrown tendency cannot further corrupt or divide me against myself and more importantly, You.

As the world reels from revelations of our collective bondage and the *lack* of freedom, as the further fallout and crises brew from the betrayal from *all* corners, this seamless interlude is staggering and heightens *why* I keep hovering this zone, or drain.

An unborn life as a people. A miscarriage of everything. We have fused too many things. We now reap the consequences of our folly.

Your Sun shines brightly upon us—You are above the tree line. You bring healing; You bring clear light needed to untangle my own blended strands of life.

Like the lame man, I have missed it. I think movement and freedom will come from external resources of some material or temporal sort. Yet it is Your Name only. Hand extended, I must take the hand, get up and walk in faith in That Name. The Substance, the Evidence. Silver and gold will not give me what I am seeking—those are the claims of infidelity. Of the infidel.

I do not want to betray Your power anymore. Plow this soil. Soften with Your grace and kindness. Amend it with what it needs for refreshing, flourishing, freedom. Help me abide in the felt knowledge that You hold me and You have not left me. You are not the betraying father, masquerading, putting on a show.

You are Fidelity.

Thank You for not allowing me to bootstrap myself using my creativity and my vocation. Thank You for purifying with Your Sun. *Healing unto wholeness* so that I will not unknowingly betray You or myself, producing enmity. This was our origin story, after all. The generational curse. May it end with me.

Do not be conformed to this world (don't run with the herd), but be transformed by the renewing of Your mind.

You shall not follow a crowd to do evil.

Do you not know that friendship with the world is enmity with God? Whoever therefore wants to be a friend to the world makes himself an enemy of God.

The world is passing away, and the lust of it; but he who does the will of God <u>abides</u> forever.

The truth is in <u>Jesus.</u>

Aspire to lead a quiet life, to mind your own business and to work with your own hands.

September 14

Trust. Affirmation.
I stop here. These are not words I care for. I disconnect them. I formidably work around them by projecting these onto others. I make a living being trustworthy and affirmational. I must be good at it.

When the fear comes in, the fearful self with nowhere to retreat, it topples me. Because survival and heroism are comfortable, love even, I find a crisis to focus on, to direct my fear as strength, to relive the fight-or-flight. Likely, I concoct the crisis to head off what could be the larger pending crisis. Time on my hands is not necessarily best. If I am to be a *good* inner parent I will need to do *better* to provide more consistency for my safe inner Garden, like this one, to flourish. I am too used to the intensity of spontaneity that, although I am doing better, there is room for improvement.

The crickets hum in the late-Summer humidity. But the birds are rather quiet. They are waiting for Your Sun to crest the tree line.

Perhaps it is okay for the child to flit from book to book. Perhaps she is starved for freedom to color here and there without pressure of completion. She is distractible. A caring posture would be to give her space for that. I should stop pressuring her to create for your survival. She refuses—that is not her job. She has been both buried and exploited for long enough. In fact, you have exploited her a bit, or so she feels that way, because of how you have removed the comfort of her dark cocoon. The light is still harsh for her; she is not able to retreat because her cocoon disintegrated when you *rescued* her. Her light eyes are still adjusting to this brightness.

The mockingbird's urgency causes me to lift my head and the heron crosses the Garden behind the cedar's spire. You send me the creature I most long for but have almost forgotten. She flies alone today. She usually does. But she is most content that way. Such kindness and a reminder of Your trustworthiness. I need this now, I always have, and I need Your ability to cooperate with this trust.

The mockingbird lands to pick the grass just next to me. She looks at me knowingly without fear. Perhaps I have been her all along. Singing everyone else's song but my own. The troupe in the cedar, they are quiet with agreement.

Rarity. Affirmational. Trustworthy.

dis-integrated

You, even You, are He Who comforts me.

September 17

A vulture welcomed us this morning from the pulpit-perch of Osage Orange. Totem decides to sit against me. I am his backrest.

I came to the Field with agitation of a familiar kind. I try to stand erect in it as my reading suggests. I keep moving. I sing a hymn. Singing breaks it up. It's as if it cannot coexist with the frequency, vibration, lyrics. *I need Thee every hour...*

The dew hangs on the grass like diamonds. A carpet before me, needing no Sun to sparkle.

I appreciate greatly my readings. They are ever a comfort; they speak the words I know, but forget to remember.

The vulture comes on a day when the flesh on the corpse of my former dying-off life decides to make itself known. This is obvious to me.

To claim my part in the community I need Your clarification. My former restlessness or weakest self wants to wrest control from the surrendered quiet pose. She is exposed, raw, and impatient. She wants a sabbatical. She wants to be indulged. But she instead strives and toils; that's all she knows.

I have a long weekend. Sometimes these throw me into a tailspin or a setback. There is so much to do on the home front. Yet I need rest, reading, some study, maybe a little writing. Continued exploration, some gardening. Time with animals. No forcing.

I hope some of the blankness I feel is on the way to something. Sometimes I worry about this. Yesterday, I found more writing of dad's in his little Bible that I carry now and this floors me. Even this confirms.

I genuinely need Your loving assistance. Guide and order my day in the Name of Jesus. Help me to stay on the straight path and not dislocate my healing, lame limbs. Amen.

a bruised reed You will not break

You heal my broken heart, You bind my wounds

September 18

The thrasher is not happy to have me here. It ground-grumbles with its long, fawn-like tail feathers. Shy creature, it must find another hiding place.

The blue jays create a perimeter to ward off Hawk, or I can hope they sense an eagle approaching, as the flock of geese scan the freshly cut Field. The hay rounds have been moved to the border of the gravel drive. Field is wide open now, and I crave the Garden's enclosure. The family of deer takes their stand close to Amen Corner, in agreement with our premature Field exit.

By the time I arrive just inside Garden's gate, I am more settled. My agitation diminishes. I go on. I try to release the tears and complaints quickly. As the mockingbird spews its first serenade of the day from the cedar's spire, I realize the part of myself that clamors to be heard progresses through her own rotation over and over again. It is beautifully compelling as another mockingbird joins in, their mimicry is incredible. But, bereft of their own song, they urge mine to come forth. No settling for the facsimile.

I briefly look up to see the wingspan that can only be an eagle's. I focus in to be sure. Its length is unmistakable. No heron, vulture, or hawk compares. Why do You send me this now?

You have sent me eagles before. Always, always when they are most needed. Sparingly, so as not to diminish their impact. Today, I am stopped. How can You do this today? It flies over the Garden instead of the wide-open Field so I will not miss it.

No matter how my inner daughter flails, You bless and grace my seeking You here. If there were no mockingbirds would I have even looked up? Of course not. Do their songs point to the Truth of the Song? Yes. Do I have an eagle story to tell? Yes. It is Your story. Nothing else matters. You have carried me on eagle's wings out of the pit. The birds are quiet now. Their job is done. They must take their serenade to another weary soul.

From Nouwen:
I must hide the treasure and spend my energy selling my property so I can buy the field where it is hidden.

>*My future depends on how I decide to remember my past.*
>*And the rain begins.*
>*As I keep choosing God, my emotions will gradually give up their rebellion and be converted to truth in me.*
>*My restlessness is the search for God.*
>*Only when I let go of everything else can the treasure be completely mine.*
>*I am in communion with God and with those whom God has sent me. What is of God will last.*
>*Finding the treasure is only the beginning. This love must be nurtured in an intimate quiet space. If I expose prematurely, I might harm myself. Overexposure kills it.*

You are Abba, Father.
You quench my thirst
You keep me from rebonding myself to the prison of the past
You do a new thing

Sit still, daughter.

September 21

Totem and I have walked by the Garden twice because of the continual rain. Field is still beautiful and most quiet on these days.

I am beyond the walk now, and into the day, but very buoyed by what You are showing me through the words You have given me. Thank You.

You direct my hands to review all You have already given me. I need not lose heart, it is all there. I need to only *remember*.

Your Sun peeks through these days of gray and the leaves no longer hold their places on the branches. The seasons are indeed changing, bringing more and more change within and without.

The Counselor, I forget this Name, will speak only what He hears, and He will tell you what is yet to come.

I feel You are doing and have already done this. My hope is that there is enough room in my vessel to hold the Truth and then be emptied of it. Because it is daunting and does not need to be rehashed. It feels done. Whatever *it* is. Even that is still relatively unknown. I must have Your help and time to piece it together. Thank You. I feel You doing it. Guide and direct my creative movements. Help me to remember what You have already given me.

I must trust.

September 22

It rains again today as it has for the last seven days. When it lightens, we will go to the Field, but it may be too late for our Garden pause. A Fall chill has come with the drenching; I am mindful that the temperate days in the Garden are dwindling.

Sissy got outside this morning. This upsets everyone even though she is just on the other side of the fence. Her forays dwindle in length also. She realizes she is pampered with us.

I feel the pressure of the day building when I go straight into it without my sacred time. I resent the pull, the noise, the distractions. I really do. I want to scream that these all need to *shut up!*

I try to push myself into study too quickly and this also rings hollow. All I want is some solitude. I am ready for a Fall rhythm, even if I have to adjust timing or place. I miss the creature sounds and sightings. The movement that settles my restlessness. The quiet, and my trusty steed by my side, or behind, or before me.

September 23

We select another spot to sit today. A sunny patch on the grassy lawn. The vestibule to the Garden. Everything is wet from the long rain.

Sissy is still gone. Today I am in less despair. I hope she returns. I hope she is close by. I am mad at her for leaving. *How could she do this to me?* Like us, she straddles two worlds; feral and domestic. The coming Fall and the long rain kept her cooped up for too long. She took her chance. I pray she returns. She reminds me of my want to possess paired with the fear of being blamed which causes me to clutch too tightly my emptiness.

Meanwhile, as Sun warms, Totem has two eventful chases. The Herd eludes him. A group of three, followed by one straggler, emerges from the thicket and, of course, he cannot resist. He is swift for an elder. I am proud of him. He will always remind me that this sacred tending keeps us nimble. Stewing in one's own toxic stress is never healthy.

I am grateful for much. Yet, I forget to thank You. Specific provision, continued sustenance, fruitful conversations, writing encouragement. This beautiful blue Sky. Warming rays which make it possible to stay here a bit longer.

I hear machinery. This morning is too brief. Please go with me and support me in Your use of me today. Your will be done.

Thank You.

September 25

Your Sun has shifted.

To access a warmer spot we move to a wrought iron bench under the grapevine trellis. A hidden spot, even more hidden than under Osage Orange.

Totem all too easily joins me and then he asks me to reconsider. But I crave the direct rays. He feels too separate from where his nose pulls him. So I will yield.

Your Golden Orb welcomes us into the narthex of the Garden once again. Cooper's hawk clucks its invocation. Once again my insides settle in the presence of the fly that lands on my page. The traffic thrums loudly silencing any remaining crickets' whirring.

This week, my inner churning was at work. Its roiling and soul-kneading, this excavation and reintegration of former younger selves who desire reunion.

It is amazing to feel this settledness. People have departed from my life and I have yielded. Those who are meant to travel with me will.

Such beautiful weather and days. Sissy returned yesterday. Her attitude is mixed. But I feel gratitude for her homecoming. Gratitude for health.

There is an astonishing tragedy playing out in the foreground of our lives. It is challenging to believe and discern what is real. You are.

there is nothing covered that will not be revealed, nor hidden that will not be known...

I long for this because it does seem that we are collectively in the midst of profound existential turmoil. The heaviness of it wears on me. The pending crisis, the fight-and-flight of it, the need to act, versus the releasing into it. Assist. Sustain.

...grieved by various trials
...genuineness of faith (more precious than gold)
...tested by fire
...may be found to praise, honor, glory at the revelation of Jesus Christ

tribulation → fruit
perseverance → character → hope

It is good that one should hope and wait quietly for the salvation of the Lord.

The Lord is good to those who wait for Him, to the soul who seeks Him.

Wait.
Seek.

September 26

I feel a pull to face Your Orb directly. I can view it without a squint. It is shrouded in the densest fog which renders It a pure white. Its circumference clear, Its light accessible.

We enter in and the atmospheric blanket closes behind us. I keep Totem on his lead for the entire survey of the Field. For certain, the coyotes await our arrival. Of course, the hulking deer shadows will be visible at any moment. I fear letting Totem off lead. I won't be able to witness his chase. I won't be able to find him in the thicket. He kindly obliges and turns up his snout because even his sight is shrouded. We enter in because we know the way to the Garden, even though the blanket consumes all but a few feet surrounding us. I wonder more about my capacity to trust. In an unexpected way, so perfectly ordained, we must live this trust in the Field. It is our Field of play, or, our feast to consume. This truth is more than bread.

Totem decides to wander off, which is unusual, but I think he beckons me to move on prematurely today. He will find a way to wait.

I welcome the colorful, wet, dying off of Fall this year. I do not dread the shedding. I long for it. I desire the new after a period of hibernation. Root growth—deeper down is what I pray for. To give anchor to the self within to the Beyond. The I AM—the Beyond Within.

I ponder my Grandmother Joan. Her eyes are brown, but I swear they are blue like mine. The wren trills her agreement.

Help me to live this trust and experience it as I go, so that I do not mistakenly imagine that I am my own or on my own. You are with me, in me.

Now Your Orb is brightest, blinding.

Reckon myself to be dead indeed to sin, but alive to God in Christ Jesus our Lord.

If Christ is credited to me, what and Who He is is Mine. This is what I have known but must receive and accept more fully now. This is a wisening Truth.

You see...all this is yours to accept.

Thank You for softening my inner concrete with water of love and dynamite of fire.

September 27

Your Orb is too bright for my eyes today. It casts Its brightness in such a way that I cannot look directly at It, and It shines upon the Field in such a way that I close my eyes and sing and pray and let my feet guide me step by step until I reach Amen Corner and then its shade gives relief.

I can hear my father singing in my ear the Sunday morning hymns that were the music of my being. I see his stature and his shifting side to side next to me. I hear him chuckling between notes as I laugh at his tone deafness. I am the one that can sing on pitch, of course. *No wonder she hated me.*

Soul clogs, soul debris, that which I have allowed to accumulate at the behest of my self-focused thoughts, my resentment for burdens carried and carrying. I see the external realities and their frustrating hold and my weakness to deal with them, and my refusal to ask for help from my Heart of hearts, that Seat that does desire to do it Your Way...if I could only figure it out first. And, how? Default to the fusion of my worldly aspirations. I want what I want for You, but only if I can have this, and this, too. The things that accrue and stifle and overwhelm. Like Totem, I need to eat some grass and throw it all up, and not return to it.

I have seen Your Sky more blue in previous times, but It is clear today. Beautifully clear. I miss the morning butterflies. The birds seem a bit quieter as Your Sun rises later now.

Hawk greeted me this morning from Coyote Corner. Its screech is unmistakable as it traveled to the maple in the graveyard to break up a melee between a gang of crows and another hawk, or so I think. This is what You do at just the right time: when the world seizes upon our shadow and we are overwhelmed, You will swoop in and carry us on Your wings, but in Your time. You allow the crows to consume the deadness first. *Wait. Seek.*

Help me to obey, to hear and follow Your direction when I don't understand. I feel some prompting to explore some things quietly, on my own, with You. Soften my stubbornness, clean and bind my wounds so that I do not dislocate my lame limbs. Thank You for sustaining me when my flesh has been active in corrupting ways; while I think I am doing Your work, I am serving my flesh.

O Lord, You are my Father; I am the clay and You are the Potter; and all I am is the work of Your hand. Do not be furious, O Lord, nor remember my iniquity forever, indeed, please look—we are all Your people.

September 29

Dueling mockingbirds greet me—their cacophonous repertoire fools the ear. How many are there, really?

I knew this might happen. The light changes with the season and so does our timing. Yesterday we bypassed the Garden, and now there is a construction project beginning at the start of the cedar-lined drive. Cooper's hawk directs my attention to it and I wonder how things will continue to change.

I have thought more actively about visiting my mother. Things about that feel more urgent. I said the other day that I did not want to look back at this time and realize my fear had inhibited me. A very loud crow caws his agreement. Since I associate them with shedding and dying off, I need to shed this part. About this I am not clear, just that it seems important for me to look into my next steps.

Just recently I used anger, or, better, expressed fresh anger to address familiar strategies that have wearied me. I faced conflict with love and strength and I closed with confession, which was different in a way that surprised me. I felt exhilarated, clear, open. Something has shifted. I am no longer afraid.

The problem with missing a day here is that I feel a bit removed from everything. The writing, my senses. So I pause and survey. This helps.

I would love to be in a pose that allows whatever newness You want to show me to reveal itself. The pending items, I give them to you in more trust that You can and will do in and through me. It is a grace to feel some relieved pressure, less dependence on anyone in my life. Fortified. Confirmed. I hope You will find me diligent with what You have given me. Please inhabit my thoughts and allow me to establish this expansive mindset upon You. No wayward self-interest. Thank You for direction. Thank You for Your loving care.

The Sun strikes me directly and I feel Its warmth.

Let your Lion and Lamb freely and fearlessly lie together. The more I feel safe as a child of God, the freer I will be to claim my mission in the world as a responsible human being.

The more I claim that I have a unique task to fulfill for God, the more open I will be to letting my deepest need be met.

Kingdom of Peace.
Peace be with you.

September 30

My fear completely overtook me yesterday. It fashioned a crafty yarn which absorbed multiple hours. The false narrative had me awake at 3 a.m. I couldn't rest until I had greater clarity. Thankfully, Your kindness and time showed me my error. While I am back on track, I am tired and need to collect myself.

The hum of a crane around the corner. The beginning of a project. Everything changes, always.

Except, Your Sun rises and my steed remains my constant companion.

I have had full days. The continual hungering and lingering. Considering new things. Mostly that I need Your guidance as You must captain this ship into new waters.

The mockingbird tunes up her concert for the day. The dizzying transitions from song to song, so precise but not her own. I cannot default to another's song. I must sing my own new song.

This has been an incredibly fruitful month in ways that I cannot hold. The Garden creatures are hidden, quiet. They know Fall is upon us now. They know it is different here. I miss the morning butterflies.

Please continue to guide, direct, shape, protect. Let me not fall prey to the wiles of this world. Assist me in all things.

Thank You.

OCTOBER

October 2

Workers have infiltrated the grounds adjacent to *my* sacred Garden. The light changes our timing. There are often walkers. I must flex to find another spot. Amen Corner welcomes me. It offers a different perspective. No less beautiful, just more buggy. I scan the crest in the middle of the Field for other walkers bound to approach on this humid October morning.

I hear a towhee and a robin chatting with her young, or so I imagine. We are enclosed by the thicket which borders the streams that flow to and from the Harpeth River nearby. I have missed my time here each morning. It has become essential for emptying and creating space for infilling. The light keeps changing and the transition of seasons is jarring. I want to write here while I can.

For the moment, though, I am out of words. Perhaps preoccupied. Feeling as if I am late into the morning and necessaries wait. And this spot is different. More exposed, less contained, harder to relax into my center.

I bid adieu until tomorrow, I know it will be quieter.
Thank You for all You are showing me.

Of His own will He brought me forth by the word of truth.

In the beginning was the Word...

October 3

This is the first morning in a while that I have had peace in the Garden; the mockingbirds begin their call-and-response as soon as my pen hits the page. They greet me, they know I am here.

My timing changes with the late light. A construction project alongside *my* spot will likely hamper *my* quiet time here and I am sick about it. Of course, I thought *my* time would be unencumbered by anything but weather. It seems that noise creeps in everywhere these days.

This onslaught of wickedness is not greater than You. Be not afraid, take courage, endure. The suggestion of what could be and is transpiring is shocking. And yet, not. We have all gone our own way. Your breeze picks up—it brings a reminder of Comfort. I have not felt this in a while. Whether a few days ago, or a week, it feels far too long. A rain shower comes and urges me to move on. But we wait it out easily under Osage Orange's cover. I am grateful because I don't want to move. My restlessness settles here. The wind picks up. Each passing shower moves quickly and the leafy canopy holds.

It dawns on me that I am about to complete another notebook. What would You like me to do? Am I closer to claiming my unique presence? Any closer to that? Not sure. It seems You are putting things in place while providing support for this portion of the journey.

I have been talking lately about our home and how it can feel more like a home, even in the midst of life's turbulence.

Small moves for slightly more comfort. But as I sit and write this, I back out of this a bit. Maybe the inner restlessness knows that peace in anything aside from You is not possible. Being grounded enough in this reality seems paramount, however. Untangling the fusion once again.

Thank You for Your Spirit Wind and my trusty steed, whose face grows whiter by the day. My fear regarding missing Your plan for me creeps in. Allow me to yield and understand that it is happening all the while. I should not expect some grandiose arrival to appear suddenly on the horizon or around the corner.

May Your will be done through me.

May Your Spirit assist in clearing room for more of You in me.

If I speak, let me speak as an oracle of God.

October 4

I do not own this Field. But I want to. I want to possess it terribly. This is the whole point. What is mine is mine for a season. I must hold loosely and hold fast at the same time. I must endure the releasing.

I come to a spot near Coyote Corner. The mosquitoes are voracious and the tall grass in the thicket has been flattened by the deer that slept here last night.

My walk has been completely overtaken by distraction and sorrow as I am now on another's daily timeline and the walker seems always here, especially on the days when I anticipate arriving first. Then the fluorescent shirt of a crane driver corresponds to the beeping that I hear near the cedar drive. He is moving the hulking machine just outside Garden's fence and I am forced elsewhere. Gratefully, the workers are quiet for a moment. I can hear the crickets, the finches. Ten geese squawk my way as they fly over. Totem returns to my side aware of a greater expanse to survey. The humidity fogs my glasses in un-Fall-like fashion. It seems par for the course. Nothing is as it should be; yet, all is well at the same time.

This is not the change I am seeking. The respite You have given is slipping away and I am heartsick for a home that I am not sure I will ever have in this existence. I am fairly certain that You want me to release that as well. This is not my home. This is not my Field. But I so want it to be.

I return to my spot after Totem runs off to protect me from another walker. I hear him say how scary Totem is and I scream in my head *Yes...this is why I am here and why I go to the Garden—to be left alone!* Maybe I can tuck into the back Field. But I think this is temporary. It's all temporary. We are just strangers and aliens passing through.

Peace—please give me peace in the passing through.

Your Sun shows Itself to me in a couple of precious ways today. May You allow me to remember that You remember me.

October 5

Amen Corner calls us. As does the crow. The Garden is lost to us for now, and the colors continue to change.

Double-minded doubter, you are unstable. In or out, which is it? Thinking, thinking. Rest periods consumed with information. How much more do you need?

I must wait on Him, doing business. What is real? What is trickery? Trickery on the *good* side no less. So much more to do. So much more. I come back to quiet stillness and try to remember. Yet, when my timing is off, like today, I flail and flounder.

The Field is my reality. I breathe it in. When I doubt I set myself up for the *rejecting* way. When I am fooled, I feel like an idiot, and then I beat myself up. Like Your power in me will be stolen by the tides. Untrue. This just reveals the shallowness of my belief, and *this* reveals that perhaps my time believing in, and embodying Your Love, has been so very brief. I think of Your temptation, how much was before You. You saw and felt it all, yet You were Faithful, You were True.

The hum of traffic is louder and louder.
Modern voices I don't want to hear.
I want to hear You.

I am sorry for my wavering. Help me. You tarry because of Your longsuffering towards those who will still remember You.

Back to the land—row—stop peering into the deep as if you are capable of understanding. This is your folly. Trust Me, dear Daughter.

There is no trickery, no *gotcha*.

From Nouwen:
You have found the treasure but are not ready to own it
let go of everything else
I am on a search for what I have already found
I can only seek God when I have found Him

lovingkindness, faithfulness

nurture this newfound love in a quiet intimate space

Finding the Treasure without being fully ready to own it will make you restless.

October 6

Your Sky is staggeringly beautiful. Beyond description. Construction is quiet. Other walkers are absent and I am convinced You have set this ethereal table for me today. You knew my hunger for it, my desperate need. I pray for time to slow to be here. *It does.*

It seems I have missed the most important thing. It is notable that those I do care to read don't dwell here either. Those to whom I relate tend to strive with me. Yet, it hits me like a bolt. The Endless Abiding is the complete yielding to my true Parentage and Your choice of me, Your sacrifice for me. Your Love of me, which frees me.

I am Yours, I am Daughter.

Perhaps I have written these words long ago. Perhaps the younger me knew this once but forgot to remember. Perhaps all the props had to fall away so the Field could be open and clear enough to find this Treasure. It is about trust, but not in a way I have understood it. It is about Your Loving Fatherhood, and Your delight in me.

I have suppressed what felt loving about dad. There is absolute, unequivocal truth that he loved me. In fact, I think he was lost and often lost without me. I think I was his anchor. Yes, we were enmeshed; yes, he exploited me. But, he was the truest family love I knew and likely will ever know. I was fiercely loved by him, I was his joy. Thank You for this sacred reckoning. If I allow myself to imagine him, miss him, grieve him, he becomes the bridge to You, and he doesn't have to remain bones in the ground.

The Sun bursts through. Your Sun, Your Light radiates in full agreement.

How can I not thank You?

As we depart and pause at the Garden gate, an eagle flies directly over my head. *Of course.* It flies to the middle of the Field, its span unmistakable. It turns left and I lose sight of it in tree tops of the cedar-lined drive—but I know it came for me, undoubtedly. What a gift. Utmost communion.

Essential reckoning → Emancipation → Endless Abiding

I am Your child
I have a Brother to show me the way
I have Your Spirit
which to my death and beyond indentifies me as Yours

The mockingbirds scream their songs in Your Sun's Light.

October 7

It is unusually quiet. There is no traffic noise. How is this brief serenity possible? *Thank You.*

I request that Totem pause with me under the maple which overhangs the graveyard. It protects the fence from the pervasive lichen patina. I am struck by the quiet. The silence is so welcome. Like pure water to my soul. This tree is Hawk's perch, yet, I have not seen any Red-tailed friends for days. I now remember the blonde-headed one perched on the cedar spire looking at me sideways. I tuck myself away just enough so as not be interrupted. I am touched by this silence only broken by the geese's honk and the squirrels' chatter.

The Treasure in the Field: the Child that You love who wants to endlessly abide in the embrace of this peace. It is too fleeting and I ebb and flow in and out of it always.

Root choice: to remain by the power of Your Spirit of adoption that cries out within me. To cry out often for a steering Hand of assistance. To wait patiently for it. To trust the Eagle will come to swoop down and carry me to refuge. To do business in the meantime.

To hear only birds is a generous sequel to yesterday. I dare not dig up the just-planted Seed. I must believe it landed in good soil and wait patiently for it to germinate and sprout. In the meantime, the details of life beckon to me and for those I desire Your guidance. You are a loving Father who would and has done anything and everything for me. This is not hyperbole, this is reality.

You are *for* me. Such gifts of goodness.

Amen.

October 8

Your Sun warms the bend at Coyote Corner. We rest here today. The hum of life is ongoing. We relish today and anticipate the quiet of Saturday and Sunday in the Garden. I am fatigued but contented. Grateful for Your abundant provision. Your care.

Rumors of war, and actual war, abound and unfold. I anticipate my temptation to be sucked in to manage the inevitable catastrophes, as if that's possible. Fear. My thinking travels to this: *What if I did nothing?* I am not sure I know how to hear from You in this urgency. Certain items seem important. As I write, I wonder why I might *conjure* that You don't care about these very things. Why are we imprisoned by this survival?

Like Totem, I turn and face the thicket to hear and see the birds. To absorb Fall's colors like Your Sun's warmth on my back.

My mind is tired. Likely I will not think clearly today. I could have lowered energy. I may need a nap. To sink into some rest.

Consider the lilies, the birds of the air. You provide for them. They have no thought of provision.

The robins fly together, tipping their wings in concert to feel the warmth on their feathers. The *chit chit* of the finches, the trill of the cardinals.

I cling to this life because it is what I know, or what I think I know. Perhaps I fear never feeling these things. Hearing Your birds, seeing the blue Sky, being annoyed by my animals. Driving to work, hearing Bruno's guitar play.

Seeing the green grass. All of these things. Such a special place You have given us. Help me to treasure it without clinging.

You are showing me things that help point me to You. Please give rest and guidance at the same time.

Barnabas (son of encouragement) <u>*sold a field*</u> *he owned and brought the money and put it at the apostles' feet. He had found the Treasure. He claimed it and sold his possessions and gave it all to You.*

October 9

I miss the herons. The hawks. Each morning I scan the tree line for them, to no avail. Their new perches are hidden to me. The mockingbirds, ever present, are pleased by their absence. The workers and walkers are also absent, therefore, the Garden sanctuary is ours.

A hazy, cooler Fall morning. Attempts at inhaling, receiving the pure air from Your trees and grass and foliage. Still green, still lush—likely not for long.

More than sparrows, ravens, grass, lilies. Do not seek after all of the things that You know I need. The wren trills incessantly. Your Orb is about to peek over the tree line. You mortar my cracks with gold and silver-spun gossamer pressed into the hovels where shame used to reside and encrust.

After a time, after my own attempts to clean and clear, the recognition of daughtership takes hold. That is where my child waits, the one who has been buried in performance, expectation, responsibility, disappointment, and exhaustion.

This day, the Day of the Lord. Not man's, not even wickedness has any power, except what You allow. You tarry to bring more Home. This Day cannot be managed by me. My needs are in Your hands. In You I seek refuge. Only You have the power to dim the Sun.

Mockingbird flits from Osage Orange to cedar spire. This close, she screams at me.

I am daughter. You are Father. This is the beginning of everything. The geese honk their approach. The woodpecker warms itself at the top of the spire.

I am daughter
created, yet
a masterpiece beyond measure
a priceless, unique being
fashioned by the Craftsman

But, I am daughter
chosen for fulfillment
cracks and all
mortared by gossamer,
gold and silver

do not let me falter
by our incoherent visions
You are unbound
our finitude cannot process
Your Fullness of time

Like sheep we are herded into
a vast pasture
of fraudulence
it is a wide gate
available to all
alluring
but not Your Gate

Your Gate is a Beautiful Gate
but it is hidden
covered in brambles
a narrow, winding way
with little assurance at first
a solitudinous beginning
followed by an arduous climb

I am suspect of all
I have never traveled with the herd
I will not start now
Mary, Sister,
walk in her footsteps
read her words
find her good part
If He is Son
She is daughter

October 10

Your Sun greets us through the cleft in the tree line. We select our spot in the Garden accordingly, we cannot get enough. Freed from his harness, Totem lies down beside me easily. This truth is not lost on me. Even upon these grounds, this Field, the yoke of our times is heavy. The narrow gate is heavy. The way to tread is difficult. Yet, Your Strength in me is also unbound. I may bind it, but I try with Your help to give it more room.

I seek the hawks in the tree line but I receive the raven. You provide nonetheless.

In this season of upheaval, I ask for an eye to see Your Kingdom within and Beyond. I ask for the ability, Your ability in me to speak truth with integrity of heart, soul, mind, Spirit, and unity to those You send to me. That the simplicity of You would be evident and Life-giving to all You want to hear, see, know.

The delusion: that a better world *here* is coming in. A collectivist construction. A fusion of faith and material. You defied the collective knowledge. You came to the poor in spirit. You knew the little flock would multiply. Your Kingdom is Beyond; but it is within, and is always a reversal of our worldly wisdom without.

I am daughter. You have been with me all the while. I will follow. Please allow my being to hear, see, know. Uncover the truth within by Your Spirit. Allow Your Light to shine brightly through. Help me to be a vessel of use for Your cause.

The world is passing away. It will never be as it was; it is changing even now. A longing for otherwise is futile.

To be the hopeful stranger and alien, and savor the present gifts is my aim. Forgive me for tasting the falseness of the world, with ever the justification for it. To fix my eyes on You; that is the continual goal. There are massive happenings occurring. Beyond comprehension. Grant the tools for enduring. I want to do Your business.

You know my heart to do Your will which You have and will equip me for. Be the energy that propels me forward. Be the peace that allows me to rest.

Thank You.

Writing calls, Scripture responds directly. Thank You.
Romans 8—adoption vs. slavery of spirit to bondage of fear

That in the dispensation of the fullness of the times He might <u>gather together</u> in one all things in Christ, both which are in heaven and which are on earth in Him.

whoever wants to save his life will lose it

October 11

I flail and falter once again. Grateful for the holiday which keeps our Garden sanctuary free of workers. We have a schedule to keep. I ask that You slow time.

Crows abound; no hawks. Fall's light and breeze are beautiful. The foreboding hides in the shadows. It resides in my torso. It clenches as Your breeze invites me to breathe. Thank You. It comes at the exact right moment. I know it as You.

I consider the remainder of the month—Your breeze tells me *no, let it go, release. It's arbitrary what You are thinking. Bondage unto fear.* The wren chortles in agreement.

My memory is challenged, and Your breeze tells me to quiet my mind. It is very breath. Totem bonks me with his arm. He wants his scratches. This is what matters, of course. I rest my head on his hindquarter and try to embrace this second, this moment, and I pause—just to see what's possible.

I need Thee, oh I need Thee.

The Lord is near to all who call upon Him. He will fulfill my desire, hear my cry and save me.

I will not leave you as orphans, I will come to you.
I am with you always, even to the end of the age.

I am not a prisoner, but a <u>daughter.</u>

Thank You for the breeze that enshrouds me.

October 12

I come to the Garden despite the cranes, the workers, the beeping, the laughter. We sit under the arbor. The arborvitaes protect us from view.

My prayer: that in spite of my inner storming, that I have been a good steward of the gifts and the grace You have given me. I pray the storming is part of the purification, the message of integrity in a healing vessel. The readiness. Prepare my heart for what You have for it. Knit it all together. You are.

Thank You for this secluded spot and what it gives me. Please continue to guide and direct my steps. You know what we need when we need it. Thank You.

I am daughter.

Sovereign Lord,
You made the heaven
and the earth
and the sea
and everything in them
(including me)

October 13

I am at the beginning, or the end. The spoilage of our times has come to my Sanctuary and I complain the whole way around. The workers focus on the other side of the house. Their beeping cranes are constant. The sprinklers turn on and I realize my time is short. Extend time, please.

Tents and trailers infiltrate our Sanctuary. This enrages me. Yet, still, Osage Orange holds my place and Your breeze picks up.

I am daughter, I am lamb, I am child. I am not made for wrath. Such remembrances are crucial. *Do business 'til I come.* Back facing the Promised Land. Row. Jesus' Name; faith that comes through His Name creates healing. Your joy is the balm. Your goodness gives it all to and for me.

The mockingbird in the arborvitae sings to the one on the spire. It is time for song, repentance, humility, confession, request, praise.

Why do the nations rage and conspire against Your anointed?

It will not stand.

If any are here for this, it is our destiny. Love not my life, for that I will lose. I am not of this world. I am here to flavor it. The plane cannot drown out the mockingbird cantata. Creation bests machine any day, any time.

I am Yours, I walk forth. I am open to Your charge. Reveal my path. Help my feeble bones to stay upon its narrowness. You have made a way for me. My soul cries out. *I need Thee every hour.* Every moment. Every second. Every breath.

October 14

In spite of the cranes and the hazy sky, Your beauty shines through and the late-Fall lilac blooms greet us at the Sanctuary's gate. I am without my Bible this morning and that causes me to wince. I know how much I need Your Words and also, I know that there is a shift this week that I want to acknowledge, because I cannot maintain on my own strength.

Your Sun rises later and later. The colors are showing ever so slowly. There is peace in the settling and satisfied appetites. Answers to prayer.

Right now I feel my writing is confined, perhaps due to where I am in this journal or the incessant crane beeping. Both. Not as free flowing. Irritation. I can't even think with it. Two more days until the weekend. Those will be my quieter days. The noise is painful. I am trying to wait it out. Challenging.

The Kingdom of God is within, not without. It suffers violence. You tarry for more to come in. Always things to do, pulling me outside of this inner Home.

The *chit chit* of the cardinals. The caws of the crows. The duo on the grass. The towhee that welcomed me first today.

Peace.

October 15
Richie's Birthday

> *Rich,*
> *How we have grown.*
> *How have we grown?*
> *I feel a wholeness coming on, taking place. A unifying communion. A bite of this Bread fulfills like the ravens that fed Elijah. It is a feast—not a crumb. It multiplies to the thousands of splintered parts that have been gathered into the baskets of His Arm. His Branch. His Vine. Or the baskets were woven with generations, even epochs, of Vine. Therefore, they hold the sharp but tender edges that need binding and mending together.*
> *This I know now. It's a knowing throughout my vessel. It permeates all of me. Nothing withheld.*
> *I am daughter.*
>
> *I believe we were both struggling to retain this knowledge. Our parents, even as they tried their best, could only point us to Jesus by their frailty.*
> *He is our Brother.*
> *He is our Father.*
> *The Spirit tells me so.*

October 16

We struggle to find a Sun-filled spot in the Garden. It is at once Fall; its chill a sudden reminder that our sacred morning times in the Garden may not be as easy on us. I am grateful to witness Your Sun's rise with Totem; we are both bundled in our jackets. The family of deer greets us at Amen Corner. No hawks, but a flock of vultures, the same from yesterday. I think they fly together in formation close to the graveyard. In this Fall light it is easier to look at Your Sun directly. I am sure we cannot even imagine the good it does us to see It this way.

Your breeze is refreshingly cool, removing the long, late-Summer humidity. The peace You have installed remains. With it, the joy has come. As has easier breath, optimism—aaaah...hope, that's a better word for it. *Like calves released from their stalls,* I see joy in Totem's playful chase across the Field, reinforced by the deer. They mimic each other and point me to my own soul.

This daughter wonders if this chapter of restlessness is closing. As the breeze slows, I wonder if You agree. Is it time for a new rhythm? Is it time to give account for the gracious loving-learning You have wrought in my soul? Perhaps.

The urgency of our times has proven a stark contrast to the slowing I have felt, the quiet I have craved, the lifting of perspective, the lightening of load. The inner tension has dissipated, the contentment of soul is like nothing I have known, it is beyond description. Your ways are always higher; yet, You give me words to record, to bear witness to the completeness, the perfection, oneness, communion, at-one-ment versus wholeness, although it *is* wholeness. It is an inner completion. I do not feel walled off to You.

I am daughter, Chosen child of the Most High God. The God of Abraham, Isaac and Jacob, Father of Jesus Christ. Your Spirit tells me so in groans and utterances beneath and beyond my ability to scream and claim my true heritage. The Beyond Within. My True Father.

Be strong and of good courage. Be not afraid. For the Lord your Father God is with you wherever You go, Joshua 1:9. This is where and when You first came to me 45 years ago. According to Grandpa Cheatle's handmade plaque: *'God careth for you'*, I understood and accepted.

I hear the Red-tailed's *cluck clucking* as she flies overhead to tell me *yes, this is so*. The first sighting of her in weeks; I never see her in this spot.

Thank You.

October 17

At once, Fall's frost and freezing temperatures arrive. We greet Your Sun as we hoped to. Yet, the Garden is cold and we wonder how it was ever warm enough to write there. The maple by the graveyard, Hawk's typical summer perch somehow gathers enough warmth for our pause, with an awareness that our window for writing in this sacred space is closing. Your Weather is a factor to read and respect. I have to trust that You will show me other ways to receive You in the midst of Winter's unfolding.

I am not certain, but I believe I began this season of Garden writing approximately three months ago. In the heat of Summer, we race to get here ahead of it. And now, we long for it just 90 days later, or one week later. We are all of the sudden bundled and scanning for a swath of light, for this morning light may hold some elusive warmth. How quickly things can actually change. I am not even sure I mind as much when it feels this cold.

The sirens commence with no coyote echo. Perhaps they have moved on as well. We also depart. We travel by car to a place where we will not be bothered. Yet, it does not have to be on the Field, or in the Field. This is different.

I have been released of my need to own this Tennessee Field, or possess it, as if I ever would. I do not believe that is my path. But, on oh so many days, it has been *my* Field. Truly. Now, I have found where the Treasure lies. What happens to the Field when the Treasure has been found? Is it sold? Released? Are the proceeds donated so other cultivators of Seed and Field and Fruit can bring it to harvest? Possibly. *Think Barnabus.*

What seems clearer now is that I have been graced with a new understanding of my kinship, my daughterhood. I do not need a Field to remember this reality now, although I love the tempo of its reminders. The many years of longing, searching, pleading, have been answered and are answered still, day by day, regardless of the Field of play. The Sun shines brightly and I close my eyes in rest and return. My steed sits behind me, patiently waiting. As You have. I have not words for what this is. Peace? Hope? Love? Contentment? Joy?

My heart knows. I love You, Father.

October 18

My sadness travels with me in spite of Your Sun's rise—which, as usual, is breathtaking and giving at the same time.

Why sad, daughter?

Because this precious season is changing and I am fearful of returning to old fears and habits. This is new growth. Did I overexpose it? Potentially. Can it recover?

It is as much about the weather. It will soon become too cold to do this the way we have. As the leaves turn and descend from their branches, the noise will get louder and louder. If I fight it, my attitude will suffer and sour. I do not want to release this though. I cling.

its weight and weather

its need to expand

The Unknowable Fullness. Also from my reading, *are you really ready to expose this new shoot and claim your unique presence fully?* No, not yet. And with this *mean-time* comes an inner tension. Being here was a known quantity. My imagining is for a lesser situation, not a greater.

I went back to the beginning of this short journey to review a bit. I think I thought I knew where this was heading and when it would conclude. Indeed, something different and greater has been translated to me through this dailyness. Many lessons I have learned. Finding a Field with a Garden was the beginning of finding where the Treasure lies within.

Over the past couple of days, I have prayed for order. With an awareness that Your Spirit prays through me more of what I need. Always. This, too, is new. I feel sick with worry that I have missed something or failed You. This fear is old in me. Please console me and quiet me. Bring the order that may also bring some serenity. Not even ease. Peace. More tranquility. Less clutter in my soul. I get overwhelmed by the more that there is to *do* or *be*. Help me with this. My heart longs for what You have for me. Thank You, Abba.

Consolation. Faithful. True. Witness. Yes. Amen.

October 19

I write from the car.

The Field is alight with Your Golden Sun. I watch it rise from the crest of the Field with Totem. It calls to me.

We pass by the Garden, all shaded, dewy, and chilled. I know I will be back, perhaps over the weekend. I greet it with heart-panged fondness and gratitude. Our time has helped me find the Treasure. I am sad, but empty. If I wrote from there right now, very little might surface. This is not fear. It feels more like completion. And all I can say is thank You.

from, Your daughter
with a Love she has only begun to know

I wait on the Lord, my soul waits and in His Word (Jesus) do I hope. My soul waits for the Lord more than those who watch for the morning. Yes, more than those who watch for the morning.

October 20

I write from a breezy, grassy patch at my office. A surprise, midday respite to compensate for the lack of Garden time these past couple of days. This grieves me, and in a way, a small way, relieves me because it feels like change. A monarch butterfly greets me upon arrival, so I must be in the right place.

Be doers <u>and</u> hearers. My hearing lacks, or, it too is changing. It is a present struggle which I hope will resolve itself soon enough.

Now that I am just reporting, I feel somewhat blank, emptied, out of words. Perhaps this too is a grace. My tension has relieved itself and I feel lighter.

Accepted in the beloved.

October 21

I come to the Garden once again, in spite of the cranes, beeps and groans. It is balmy. I sense the winding down of this season. So we slip in and find our spot.

My reading includes pivotal verses about my standing as heir, child, daughter. *I in You, You in Me, we are One.*

The clouds fly under the firmament. The moon is full even in Your morning light. I am tucked in behind the boxwoods, unseen by workers nearby. They quiet for me; although they don't realize it is for *me*. It will be your 80th birthday soon, dad, in less than a week's time.

I dream a dream of meeting with a renowned therapist: *I bring many bags to display. I, too, am a renowned therapist. Totem is with me eating pretzels, crunching loudly, standing in the way. Protecting, attention seeking. It is a chaotic scene with books and bookcase contents askew. But she, with her blonde hair and her bright blue suit, is unapologetic. I place my written books, which I have carried, in front of her. I hold a bag in my lap and I place my head in it and sob. Many tears shed (my head in a bag? am I hiding? or, is my mind cluttered by the contents of the bag?). There is still time to sort this.*

The therapist speaks but her voice is like the lyrical speech of a loved one who knows me and also knows just what to say to comfort and direct me. Your breeze picks up and surrounds me in agreement once again. Spirit Wind, You comfort and direct.

The blonde, loving therapist speaks with kindness I need. She says she loves me and then reads my words to me and says I must write now. I get up in agreement and leave one of the bags. *My beautiful gray-leather tote. I choose not to take it with me.*

I will write. About my Daughter-self who has emerged and grounded my Being. How, by Your *Abba*-crying Spirit in me, You have helped me push back against, and clear out, the obstacles that impede, allowing me to be more fully embodied by You. I struggle, I am not perfect. But I do know *Whose I am*.

I do not want to depart this beauty just yet. There is a need to savor if only for a moment longer its fleeting. Your wind lifts more strongly. You confirm and comfort all the while.

Thank you.

October 23

Your Brightness blinds today. It is beyond lovely. Thank You for the sunny patch under Osage Orange. For the wren's song, the cardinals, the robins, the mockingbirds, the blue jays, the nuthatch, the finches. The roses, the lilacs, the hydrangea, the zinnia, the clematis vine, the grapevine. This sacred appointment is such a treasure for the depths of my being. It is such a gift.

The foreboding of this season's closure continues. Even as my pen runs out of ink, I am reminded of the transitory temporariness of it all. The mockingbird calls like a cardinal from the spire. Creation comes with us. It will not be left. This is a comfort. It has helped me release and relax even more fully into Your Grace. Why would I imagine otherwise?

Your Sun warms us both on this brisk Saturday while the traffic holds space for the crickets. What is *it?* This embodying experience of knowing that I am Yours? Your child. Your daughter. There is ease and excitement in this. What has helped me discover this Truth? Many things. Never one thing. Yet, the Oneness results and I am settled and full.

You have given me dreams. To only carry what is mine. To row my own oar with my back towards the Promised Land. To be fully present in this day is to dispatch with any pull to tomorrow or the next. Momentary questions met with *if it is Your will*. Not what I want. Yet, my trust must hold that You care about all of the minutiae and my dreams. I must pray to think Your thoughts, to dream Your dreams.

With this inner knowledge that is simply a reunion with Your Spirit within me, I am always secure. I am not enslaved to fear. I know Whose I am unequivocally and where my Home is; for I am a stranger and alien and not of this world. Neither is my Father or Brother. *The blue jays and mockingbirds confirm as Hawk appears on the spire.*

The yearning for family has been answered. You are my Family. My family claims You so we are all Family regardless of the distance on this plane. Contentment resides where the longing was; Your golden mortar of Jesus and Spirit has filled the cracks. I no longer believe I am defective because of that wrinkle in the story. Thank You is insufficient.

Oddly, perhaps, I am grateful for my father's bones resting here. It is as if You care to remind me that his presence even in this state is the tether back to You. He hasn't left me and I need not be ashamed of Your love for me even in this.

I think of you, dad. I drift to your last days. *The last time I saw you alive at home, you were crestfallen and demoralized. If I played a role in that, I am so very sorry. I had grown conscious of some need for space because family members felt threatened by our closeness and punished me for it. And you were too depleted to intervene. I was tired of carrying this burden. Perhaps this was when I gave back to you what was yours and that was too heavy to add to the weighty load already on your back. It was the final straw that broke you.*

Perhaps it was a kind of confirmation that I could live on, that you had done your job, and it was time to leave. I think aging would have been hard on you. I hate to think of the time

I saw you ashen, one year prior to your death. A conspiracy, a betrayal, a complete rejection, perhaps even by me near the end. Heartbroken. He took you, swiftly, kindly.

I love you for loving me as you did. However flawed, it was fierce. I love this way, too. Like you, it is often too much for others, and certainly flawed. But our Father loves that way towards us and with us to His perfection. I know you know this now and this soothes my heart.

You would have turned 80 in a few days. You have been preserved from seeing much that would have been unbearable to you. Your training has helped me soldier on in ways I can't even fully grasp. I carry the torch you gave me still. In honor of both of my Fathers.

Hawk clucks overhead and my pen is completely out of ink. All in agreement, it is finished. Totem turns his gaze towards me and says it's time to go.

There must be other words for *Thank You*. I do not know them.

Maybe I will sing them instead.

October 24
Sunday

I come to the Garden, not alone.
    Totem is with me; You have been waiting for me. The mockingbird in the arborvitae tells me so.

At various points we stop to meet Your Sun as it makes its climb. Pink, flame-orange, not even yellow. It refracts abundantly along the cottony edges of the pillowing clouds overhead.

I am sad. I have a new notebook and a pen. The others are full. I anticipate its ruled lines an affront to the expansive beauty of this past season. Which I presume is closing soon. But You have extended this comfort and I should rest in this present gift of a dry, mild Sunday, gifted to me and my trusted sidekick. It is one of those mornings when he can run free without second thought.

What I cannot tell, as Your breeze meets my breath, is what you intend for these months of recording these morning gatherings. When I read over them, I am convinced they are for You and I alone. This could be. I am inclined to assemble them.

I have found where the Treasure lies. I have purchased the Field. You revealed a Garden hidden to me, waiting for my presence so we could commune together as sustenance for now and not yet.

What do you want me to know by this sudden breeze that comes and goes as if it never was? Am I grasping at it?

When I reread the lines of our dialogue, our intimate conversations, I am perplexed by the richness. For a little while, perhaps since the invasion of the workers, I have experienced less solitude and even more creature-quiet in the Garden. The birds are here, but more ambient. There are no crickets or cicadas rubbing their wings or vibrating their bellies by the warmth of Your rays. The butterflies are seldom seen and the hawks have disappeared. The colors are a different vibrance. I can't quite place what it is. Like we will wait for a time for that lushness to reappear. Perhaps the hawks have moved because they don't want to face this either.

The new Truth You have helped me embody, this Beyond Within, is the reality of my standing. My True Identity. Which is only bound by Your design. Which is limitless. The grace to learn this now is also Beyond. This missing piece has eluded me for too long. I have been seeking what a part of me must have already found, but she was buried deep and needed more liberation.

The sacred present moment I now experience. It is not some mystical but seldom-felt knowledge. It is available always—and Your breeze blusters directly at my face. I know You are tracing these words or prompting my hand to write them so I can see You in their collected message.

Perhaps I am empty now. Perhaps the corners have been cleaned of their debris.

Or, perhaps You have been filling me all the while. I am not sure the difference.

What I think I know is that this Garden sanctuary is rooted within me always, but there is nothing like discovering it afresh or for the first time. The beauty doesn't fade; it is changed by the shifts of the season. While I am here, it is different. I know this place. Now it is within me. Even more familiar.

Therefore, I need this place less desperately to show me something new. The gift has been given and You allowed my hands to be open enough to receive the bounty.

Your clear Sunlight breaks through the thicket. The mockingbirds' chatter increases in volume. They are telling each other that Your Sun rises and brings them everything they need.

I lean back and can gaze directly at Your pure light. I turn to face it in agreement.

I am ever grateful for what I now understand to be the Endless Abiding.

Earlier on, I wanted to possess this place. Now I know to the depths of my Being it is already mine. Your Sun breaks through, stronger now. Thank You.

October 31
Sunday

It has been a full, wet week since I have written from here.

From Amen Corner, I spot Hawk on the spire, beckoning, welcoming me. We are on time. He leaves as we enter.

It is a dreary Fall morning, but it is warm enough to be here without a chill.

I conclude it may be one of the few Sunday mornings left in the year to be in our sacred spot with my trusty steed.

This week has held continued confirmation to which I come open handed. When rumors are entertained for too long, I desire to flee. But overnight I return to the knowing knowledge of Your care and my placement here. Like the Garden's beds, we have been cleared for a new season of growth, perhaps underground. My fears manifest through the pressing in of various needs. Yet, I know You know them all. You have given me stewardship, these are Yours.

On Friday, I visit with a guide who already has understanding of the many hard chapters of my life, so she is granted entrée to inquire, *How are you personally?* I struggle and fidget. Very few ask, and I am always uncomfortable with the question. *What about your mother?* And the quaking begins. Because there is no escaping the estrangement, rifts, and sacrifices. I rarely consider these. I consider them punishment for my actions somehow. *I am a motherless child and a childless mother.* This is the truth of it. Some doorway opens in my soul as I remember this. Those related by blood are not close to me now. The next generation and not knowing them pains me most as this childless station of mine wears on. Each one of them is an open window to my grief, like my never-grieved loss of a child who might have been. But, all of this was never meant to be.

Except this encounter reveals that I have never allowed myself to grieve these tragedies because I have held the belief close that I am destined to fly alone.

As a crow flies directly overhead squawking caws, I hear more truth: *metabolize the longing, the loss. Don't ignore it, it will become part of your wisening Mother voice and Presence in the community*, or so I can hope, as the crow pauses before me on the spire.

I shift to remember my company this week. An older therapist. We talk about You and about *Reckoning*. I claim my rootedness at a concert as I approach 30 years of life in this town and my soul resonates with every lyric out of the quintessential Southern performer's mouth.

Yes, I am still here
still standing
living through
all is well

You would have turned 80 this week, dad. This week, the week when I allowed myself to be. Here. Fully.

I am flesh on your bones
and will stand firm
and hold fast
and walk forth

And the church bells ring.

What was never meant to be
this life lived in reverse
the Blessing
a curse
of a child-turned parent
to a parent-turned child

What was ever meant to be
to inhale You in me...

NOVEMBER

November 2

Rare, this kind of clear morning. My childlike eagerness is hard to hold back from breaking out into a sprint for the Garden.

The workers are here but their beeping has not yet started. The traffic is quieter. Even the grass is dry. I decide to travel lighter today. No blanket, no pack, and the Garden unfolds dryness as a gift. My eyes and nose run from the cold. But I am giddy that I have found the Garden this way today.

I turn to face the sky where your Sun is trying to peek through. The birds are quiet but they are here. The sparrows, cardinals, thrashers, and mockingbirds. Your Sun is not high enough for their full-throttle songs. But we are close.

We sit on the grassy lawn next to the boxwoods. The openness is refreshing.

Somehow, this restful season has given me more energy for whatever comes next. I feel at peace. Sometimes awaiting the old patterns to surface. But when they do, I shoo them away like flies. I don't linger in the shame. They are pesky annoyances is all.

I have prayed for much during this season. You have, or are, answering. I am not in disbelief. I feel delight in what You are accomplishing in Your child.

I turn to Totem and kiss him, and this ushers in the beeping noisy cranes. My time is short today. But I am grateful for what it gives me always.

I am daughter.

November 3

My couch at home is not at all like the Garden. In fact, away from my sanctuary, it is difficult to ponder what I have learned. I must trust that as I revisit, and draft the entries, it will all be here.

From my couch, however, I can immediately pull up the longing and sorrow for the sweet season of abiding and flowering that has indeed passed. The growth will look different now. It is hard to imagine a way of accessing You that even comes close.

Time is irrelevant to You. Or, maybe our version of it is. As is effort, or striving to fit in time with You. But Your gift of the Garden was a place to savor first fruits of the day. There is no replicating this as Winter is upon us now. Being anywhere else is a stopgap measure. A futile attempt.

Yet, the devoted tending must continue. It is Bread, Blood and Water. It is installed so that as I write I can feel the imprint upon my heart. My throat catches, already yearning. I wonder if this is how Your creatures feel. Your plants, Your trees, before a long sleep. Going to sleep at this time seems treacherous. A vigilance seems essential. But, I know it is time to trust You as the Watchman of the night. *You will be with me in other ways.*

You are mine, You are loved, You are not forgotten.

This framed quote from *Anthroprose* fell from its shelf twice the other day. It literally knocked me in the head to confirm my learning. You travel with me, always. You are not limited to the Garden's gate or fence line.

How is it that You have given me this gift? There are not enough thank Yous. There is not enough praise. I understand why David's Psalms are lengthy; one could go on and on.

I want to record what I have learned before I forget. I am so very grateful that You have brought order to my chaotic mind and space as I have requested. Thank You for time, rest, restoration, energy, resources, peace, quiet.

Your gifts abound to Your daughter in whom You delight.

It is still dark but our clocks will shift this weekend and I will learn more about Winter's Sun rise.

November 4

Our Field is now a frozen tundra. Your Sun is bright but Its warmth remote. The grass sparkles with icy gems. I remember this beauty.

My fingers are so cold I can hardly manage a pen. There is no possibility of Garden respite and I am left to consider how to go from here and stay connected to You. Something new must come in. Just writing this causes me to ease and exhale. The flow of words is warmth. Sun within.

This unfolding season continues. You are doing something new, yet past and necessary elements remain. You must continue to guide and direct. Put the path. Do not allow me to rush ahead and sabotage or impede my own progress.

I think on many things having to do with work. So many important needs. I hope I am doing what I am meant to do. Please continue to forgive and remind my short memory about what You have already done so faithfully.

I want to serve You obediently and allow You to hew my desires closely to Yours. For me, I may envision a certain outcome, but I practice coming back to an open-handed, surrendered pose. I have little to offer, except, and because, of You.

Even today, I ask that You would continue to develop the direction. Thank You for Your grace that allows me to see and participate.

I miss the hawks. It was a gift to see the two heron fly together. She does not always fly alone.

Guide our feet into the way of peace.

November 6

The icy fog renders everything in silhouette or altogether hidden. By the time we make our rounds the eerie landscape gives way slightly to Your Sun which reveals how the leaves have turned even overnight.

Totem coughs like an aged man, which he is.

Indeed, more pages of previous chapters turn completely. Bidding adieu to previous peers and friends continues. To what end, I could not possibly know.

I am disheartened by the lack of pause and time which forged the beautiful connection I have felt. I must find another way. Please show me, even today. Keep me on Your Path. Keep my eye clear and full of light.

November 11
Veteran's Day

It seems a long time since we have visited our sacred spot. All is changing with the season. The leaves turn slowly. It is a balmy, breezy morning; we are afforded this momentary grace. Totem stands guard between me and whatever else. My pens are out of ink, my notebooks are full. Yet, I am encouraged to come today. So I bring my kit.

The Garden beds have been cleared and replanted. The litter of cranes and equipment is gone. The restoration complete. Another coincidence? Another alignment.

While I am confident in Your ability to pull me onward into further transformation, I am less confident in mine. The busy-ness or bus-i-ness of mind is like the buzz of traffic that always threatens this beautiful stream with pollution of needlessness. It is hard to send my thoughts to places that may no longer need attention. Maybe it is just time to worship in gratitude. At this, I remember to kiss Totem's whitening face. He kisses mine and paws me for a treat. I oblige as he drools on a rare blank page which will likely stick them all together, forever marking his place in this season.

The hawks hunt differently. They ride the waves of air, perhaps more keenly aware of their prey's ability to hide. Perhaps there is more scarcity to come. They still soar.

At that, I look around, surveying what has been lifeblood to me and no longer feel an urgent desperation under the surface. Is this peace? Is this contentment? Your breeze encircles me; perhaps You are all too aware of where I am heading next and all my prayers unspoken and spoken are answered there.

The Garden color has disappeared. No butterflies come to pollinate now. We produce in the hidden matter of *good soil*. Not needing the same harvest because we have stored up our understanding.

I am sure as I draft these pages I will see my soul's longing laid bare and yet I feel no need for that now. Weaned child, nourished daughter. I lay claim to my soul's contentment and comfort and will wait expectantly within this Endless Abiding.

Wherever I am, You are.

Your Word confirms and encourages this communion. And Your Sun peeks through and warms my face just as I acknowledge, this is worship.

I believe.

He led them on safely.

Let me draw near with a true heart in full assurance of faith having both my heart cleansed from an evil conscience and my body washed with Your purifying water.

November 12

Today, I feel burdened by others' burdens. There is pain and loss unspeakable in this life.

I receive more prodding and prompting to write. I sense I know what this means; when I see what has been written, I see You talking to me.

The grackles nest in the graveyard's fencepost without a finial. I am so pleased to see this today.

November 13

We sit in the car today. It is a beautiful, late-Fall morning and I continue to feel a season closing so that a new one can open.

Hawk soars yet is badgered by the crow. What is my crow? The scarcity, the familiar lack, the bondage unto fear of forgottenness. My torso tightens, and I breathe to release.

The Sun is high and warmer, the traffic quiet, the cranes gone. More verification of newness as the colors change and the bare branches expose themselves to the elements. Growth underground now.

In fact, this week delivered encouragement from a kind stranger in regards to my writing. Somehow he sees a trajectory which I experience as Your prompting. This tenderness immediately softens me, especially as earlier this week I voiced my desire to write.

My body is tired with a rare cold and I desire to soothe it with a catalog of needs that You know all about. The sparrows in the thicket tell me so.

Much shifting and settling has transpired in the past few months. Behold You are doing a new thing. Do I not perceive it? Streams in the desert. Highways in wasteland. Keep walking forth.

I pray for much. Material needs, spiritual needs. The ability through You to bring forth what is pleasing. To give others what You have given me. Your stiff breeze allows me to lay back and be carried by Your Spirit Wind which

I need so desperately as the world tremors in birth pangs. They distract, I prefer discernment of what You would have me to do next. This trust must build within the restoration. Yet, it is impossible without You.

Joy, fullness, clarity, love, prayer within this Endless Abiding.

November 14
Thesis

Five-plus years.
    The time it has taken me to complete the program, which continues indefinitely in this school. *Still, I am only a young apprentice.*

I attended this program at a Field. My tutor was my sidekick creature, Totem. He would not let me rest until I found my stride of consistency and study.

This school of suffering, as Kierkegaard may have called it, is designed to draw one inward *(suffering=lifelong learning)*. Days, years, decades of my life proved to leave me starving for this inward journey. I had perfected external interventions of all kinds, was even blessed with a meaningful vocation to support me in this quest to ignore my inmost child buried in my soul's debris.

Your call was in her and You could no longer be silenced. Or, You wouldn't be. It was past time, or, better, Your Fullness of time. I come willingly now after these years. I come for extra help, for independent study.

Even as we approach today, a deer from the Herd lays fallen. As we depart, the vultures begin to zero in upon the reason why their radar pings them from afar. They are meant to claim the flesh so the soul can be freed.

The two hawks greet us from their bordering barren tree. They survey the Field, the students, the teachers. They strike only when something is amiss. Otherwise, their guardianship is required from on high. Such sentinels.

What I know for certain is that this school saved my inner life from further extinction. I now know Your voice in me without hearing it. I understand the fullness with which You fill me. When I fruitlessly empty or spill outside of my station, I am doubly thirsty. Your faithful infilling is unmatched.

This closing season of this part of the program has been the most sweet. To feel the striving cease is miraculous. Yet, I need only step one foot beyond this Field to understand the threatening, devouring treachery that awaits this tender growth. The deer reminds me of this today. Death is ever hovering. Yet, in this school, I have come to know in the deepest recesses of my Being that death is a doorway to be welcomed, yearned for even, because it is when and where Your fullness in me begins to shape and fill me.

As I felt prompted to enter the Garden for my final semester's integration, I now feel prompted to complete the dissertation. The thesis is simple, yet never easy, and always confounding: Fear Less, Love More

How?	Find your Field
Why a Field?	That is where your Treasure lies.
Where?	It is hidden in your vessel. The innermost, buried voices of younger yous cry out to you, always hoping you will find this Treasure within after

much seeking. Jesus waits with them to bring about reunion in due time.

When?   When your Treasure trusts you are earnest in your seeking, and devoted to finding it, and knows you have dedicated everything you have to nurturing it until it can be given away. But you *must* experience Its Fullness first. You can only give this Gift out of what you have first received. It will outlast your complaints and demands to show Itself any sooner than your agreement to this.

For what Purpose?   So that you, as a created vessel, can be filled to overflowing.

So that you know Where to come when you are emptied; *to the Inner Garden and Its Master, Your Father and Maker, Who waits for you with loving delight.*

To know that you are meant to be used according to a Love Higher than your imagination and Deeper than the deepest ocean or abyss within.

So that others will know the Truth of this loving exchange, for this is their

emancipation from the fragmentariness
and desecration of a worldly life.

These are just a few of the lessons learned. You must return for more and your Maker will show you.

This is the school of daughtership; only orphans apply, for this is a learning laboratory of living and loving, guided by the Beyond Within.

This is the beginning and the end, and the beginning of everything everlasting.

Little deer,
Your herd will miss you
as we will
Your hind's feet soar
even higher
in the Presence
of Your Maker now

Of this, we are certain
By this, we find comfort

Fullness
Grace upon Grace

November 17

We cannot resist our Garden stop this morning, kit or no kit. We are greeted by Your Orb's blinding brightness, and now the breeze encircles us under the lightening leaves of Osage Orange on a balmy late-Fall, Spring-like morning. This beauty catches my breath.

How to express: A book, sent from another time, all too familiar, shows me the way. Pressed down is this abundance of knowing and utter confirmation. The seeing, the *in*seeing, the path before me, as Spirit Wind agrees.

This volume is a teacher, the author also. The riches in poverty. The claiming of true station, the not missing it, the blinding truth, like the Orb that illuminates and colors all. It pulls me into and unto Itself.

I am a pilgrim on a pilgrimage. I am a stranger, and outcast, but I am daughter of the Most High, and I am not my own. I am a vessel to be used in this time, in this place. It is my honorable service.

While the vestiges of pesky soul stains become more formidable in the worldly hours' demands, the wren's song reminds me I have had to walk the Field to find the Treasure. Her trilling, beautiful; her cunning, fierce. She devours the life of others as she woos them with her siren song. The impenetrable shell of Your covering is my only defense.

The inner movements of my soul's need to grow into greater attunement are met by You, Beyond and Within this Field and Garden. The sustenance is sweet and nourishing manna. It stems the grief of losing it, yet it is never lost. It is only found and found again.

But the aching, yearning, grasping *as the breeze blows her smile* has ceased for now. This fountainous gift only ended by Omega. And then, there is only a Beginning again.

The two hawks wait for us to pass, they absorb Your rays. They understand.

November 18

Faced with sickness, cold, snow, heat, I am rarely deterred from my Field.

Waking to rain as a Fall cold decides whether to entrench itself or depart is another concern. My trusty steed dozes while I clumsily rise to assess what is possible, only to return with my coffee, which I spill a little —typical.

But I wonder whether my two hawks wait in the barren tree even when their Sun's rise is cloaked in moisture. Whether the grackles will dive and rise from their nest in the graveyard's fencepost without a finial. They entertain the souls that reside there. Memory as transport; what a gift.

The rain has taken most of the remaining leaves. Someone told me that the Fall's leaves' colors are their true color without chlorophyll. I wonder just now what my colors would be without Yours, and if this coloring shows itself too while You take my growth underground and how this feels sad to the tree; beautifully sad.

My new volume from another time shows me a great deal. Your detailed handiwork is abundant. My feebleness finds it hard to hold. But my rising Spirit, or, Yours in me, attuning my soul, knows this is true.

My steed fidgets, he will want to go soon, until his coat is drenched. Then he will retreat knowingly. But we will still be sad together to miss our time of worship—exultant joy. There is nothing like this unanticipated gift.

Our hamlet is becoming more crowded with strangers who may or may not care about their own pilgrimages. We have called Franklin home for 30 years. My father's bones are here. There is no possible way that this is not our home. Yet, we both yearn for another, some days more than others. We struggle to know what is true about our times and mostly clear on what we are to do. Some days, the background of din and noise and decline overwhelms. The Field brings me truth, and assists me to yield and surrender to this present station which seems fruitful in many less visible ways.

We are living through a time of great reckoning after awakening from a long sleep and a painful thaw. How will we bear it? Yet if we don't, what is our part?

My reading reminds me that a century ago, these same questions were pondered by a soul who savored a Field, as I do, to ground him in his transitoriness. It is a beloved gift.

My cat comes up beside me. I settle him and nestle him in blankets. An echo of a question: *will the destination that awaits me provide such loves? Are they reserved only for here in this form? Will they travel with me?* Unknowable Fullness. An end comes before a beginning. I cannot live without the knowledge that You will meet me there despite the horrible thefts of evil in this realm which have dimmed our knowing like the ink in my pen.

These cats that find us are like those rare stray travelers who need a show of love and some food to help them on their way. Some stay, some come and go.

We love them all.

November 20

The vast spread of yellow leaves, which the maple has shed, is the blanket upon which I sit.

Totem is perplexed and I shoo him away when I should receive his precious advances; *remember, this is a waning season.*

We walk the Field first. The brusque breeze is not as chilly as it could be, but it is not until the round is complete that I retrieve my pen and sit back against the graveyard fence. The souls are *tsk-tsking* me for not behaving better with my creature. They hear my short-temperedness; they silently remind me of my place here and it reduces me to my shame and frailty. Forgive me.

The beauty of this Field still levels me, awes me. My sense of soul and body and spirit unify unmistakably here. My memory is so brittle with the conditioning of the physical that I will forget once I cross the threshold. This seems the only way to attempt remembering. *Install, daily.*

The leaves lighten and reflect the whiteness of Your morning light. I exhale. Hawk has lilted above me the past two mornings. The breeze, Your wind is stiff enough for the cuts and dives and turns. She is quietly carving her path. I am her solitary witness.

I have urgency with some things. There is much movement. I doubt my readiness, but nothing is certain and I am trying to both yield and inquire as You kindly grant confirmation in multiple forms. This loving guidance reflected upon reminds me of what my child-visitor said yesterday, *I am not alone.*

Kindly go with me today and into the necessities of material existence. Assist me in remembering that this stream that I yield into each day is the Progenitor of this new movement.

Thank You.

November 21
Sunday

Totem is jubilant to come to the Garden on this mild, late-Fall Sunday. Pockets of quietude are disrupted by traffic more easily heard through the barren thicket.

Mind-muddied with congestion, I come to recapture a sense of this season. The undoing is done, I believe. There are no more hidden knots, at least at this time. My pen does not even want to move too much.

I continue my prayers. I understand more about the distractions of our time and how they are oriented towards capturing energy, and I desire to persist against that in the way that You have designed for me.

I ask myself if I am done, but I find the cardinal in the crepe myrtle and survey the peace in this emptiness, the waiting for filling can be its own season.

Settled. I feel *settled.*

I scratch Totem to remind myself not to cling but receive the gift of this Time. Await the Master Embroiderer's continued use. Give that energy. Expectancy.

I notice his harness needs loosening. He stands before me in his regal auburn way. He is the color of the Red-tailed's feathers. *That* auburn. He is the color of the Fall leaves. I hope he forgives me for being impatient with him.

I see my aging hand as an extension of my aging countenance and hope for light, love, a piece of ground to experience You and commune.

I am a pilgrim here. As were the ones before me.

November 25
Thanksgiving

I have done myself no favors by allowing myself to run out of room in my Field notebooks. True to form, I have made things harder on myself.

Osage Orange has spread its own leaf blanket, revealing its true form. As we approach Your Garden, Your Sun captures the heart-shaped burl. You welcome us once again.

The beauty of this place is beyond my ability to describe. On a quiet, warm, late-Fall holiday morning, the gray skies threaten rain, blanketing the sky in oceanic hues, while Your white Orb refuses to be engulfed. Totem is spry and buoyant. He tears through like a pup and also refuses to be overtaken by my need to contemplate. So we play first.

The tide of these times swell. You are the Pattern, You are the Pattern Maker. You are the fulfillment of the vessel. I live in Your Field. I am Your Field. You have buried the vessel with its Treasure and I must seek, and then wait, to find It. You are and hold the map with its contours, unique to my search. I must come to You for guidance, or my searching will be futile. Remain, abide, listen to the Truth of Nature. Heed. Yield. Come in to the Garden in a surrendered pose. Expect to find.

When it is found, the Treasure within is encased in debris. Cleaning, cleansing, scrubbing it is its own effort, timely and painstaking.

The skies darken, the breeze blows, carrying voices of others.

Thank You is an insufficient phrase. Your lovingkindness to me in showing me this place and all it continues to reveal, is most often beyond my words.

What I desire, I hope and pray, is completely aligned with Your design. I await its further unfolding. I am blessed to have a chronicle of this season. There is less to observe as the falling of the leaves keeps drawing my attention to the rooting. Rootedness underground.

Mostly, the contented, settled emptiness feels like my readiness to receive whatever it is You desire for me.

Yes, says the breeze and the finch and the raindrops.

And Amen.

THREE YEARS LATER

THREE YEARS LATER

It is critical to remember the many lessons this inward journey continues to teach me; this ongoing devoted tending of the treasure that found me in my field. To return to what was recorded is to hear His Voice in the words, the power of which transcends time and reflects back these years later the work He continues to do. Even without my trusty steed, who departed for the Hereafter Abiding months ago to join other fallen sparrows we have lost. As the landscape changes with the seasons, I remain in awe of the sameness of everything. Yet this fresh heartbreak travels with me to keep me tender to my frailty.

One lesson: progress always comes as a reversal of worldly logic, for the soul is not understood by this. While reason and order are vital outgrowths of this effort, this *effort* is not *effort* as we may imagine it. Except to yield to a posture of receptivity and listening, I cannot and could not *effort* my way into further understanding of the soul and its insatiable appetite for its Maker.

While this volume includes approximately 90 entries, thereby supporting the belief that new practices require repetition to endure, an abundance of notebooks have since been filled with continued healing and learning to share.

As these notes speak from the wounded roots and reckonings discovered early in my Inner Field survey, several items recorded in this collection have resolved themselves; others remain incomplete for now. The inherent tensions are made more bearable as the healing lessons inevitably bring about the soul's reviving. Then, and only then, as the soul finds life through this restoration, does the pathway to purpose and true fulfillment reveal itself.

This is also true: the hushed Word in the stillness is the soul's mother tongue. There exists a dialect unique to each of us, for the Word is infinite in its imprint and expression upon the Inner Field. Its fullness sustains through waves of sorrow and struggle; these also remain as constant material for our transformation in the Potter's hands. There is no formula, no quick fix to quench our deepest longings. A solitary stillness as a way of being is the essential ingredient for the only conversation that satisfies to begin. Within this inner dialogue, I sense the delight of my True Father as He guides me to yield even further to this consuming devotion. It is all I have that is worth this living through. And, dearest reader, it is everything.

As our human family continues to grapple with the paltry sums that result from the deceit of self-attainment and emptiness of material pursuits, the Father's storehouse supplies an ongoing feast for our souls' nourishment. This communion within the most hidden rooms of your being where the hearth of the flame of Life Everlasting burns steady and bright awaits your return to be settled in by the Comforter.

May you find your Field and the fullness of its treasure. May it sustain you for your inward journey, for while the outer winds of turbulence taunt and swirl, of this I can assure you, they are no match for The Endless Abiding.

ACKNOWLEDGMENTS

DEDICATION

This collection is an offering of thanksgiving to the I AM that I AM, the Most High God of Abraham, Isaac, Jacob, Moses, and David, for His loving Fatherhood, which He has kindly extended to this adopted daughter. While You are beyond any name, You must be named.

It is presented as a Book of Remembrance to Jesus Christ of Nazareth, the Savior and Son of Our Father, Who remains my Hero, Teacher, Brother, Friend, and so very much more than my narrow vocabulary can express. By the power of His creative Word and healing Name, my daughtership is sealed.

May it serve as a testimony to the Helper-Counselor-Comforter-Spirit of this Truth, Who infills my soul with guiding Light upon its sojourn Homeward; Whose very Substance sustains this Endless Abiding in the Mean Time.

IN MEMORIAM

This volume is given in remembrance of the sparrows that fell during its completion: Isabel, Zak, and Sheila.

To my beloved companion and canine tutor who shared his unwavering presence with me before departing for the Hereafter Abiding: I listen for you each morning; I sometimes hear you in the Wind that blows upon our Field.

Cynara's Checotah Autumn Colors
'Totem'
09.10.2010 ~ 10.22.2023

WITH GRATITUDE

My hometown of Franklin, Tennessee, has become a chosen family member to me as I have lived the entirety of my adult life within its quiet neighborhoods. To have found my Field here is a gift for which I will be forever grateful.

To those who have generously read this volume or invited me to facilitate their Inner Field work during its completion, alongside close friends and family members who offered support without knowing I was taking this journey, I am thankful for you and lovingly hold you in my Field prayers.

Kevin Norwood, your attentive tidying of an early manuscript contributed greatly to its final form.

Carol Lynn Rivera, your steering editorial hand wields a scalpel of precision. Heartfelt thanks to you and Ralph M. Rivera for your friendship, contribution to this project, and tireless efforts on my behalf.

Tracy Steinle, thank you for your wise intuition to take a sabbatical as this is the fruit of that rest. Andrea and Corey Smith, your friendship, tenacity, and last-minute insights propelled me across the finish line of this work's completion. Kelly Dougherty, your timely consolation brought fresh waves of perseverance. Kim Fournier, thank you for walking this Field of Life with me and for being a loyal Auntie to Totem. Rachel Corum, your belief in me, and our pockets of rest together water my soul.

To my cousins Kim and Jeff Stone, thank you for your thoughtful early reading and meaningful feedback.

Scott Norton, you are more brother than cousin; thank you for your faithful encouragement of this project and for your loving, enduring friendship.

Bruno, you are family of my heart. Our life together with our brood of cats provides respite from the strain. Your support and fierce care surpass description.

NOTES

Two inspirational resources traveled with me to the Field and Garden each day to play a steadfast role throughout my healing-unto-wholeness journey: Samuel Bagster, with Anne Graham Lotz, *Daily Light for Every Day* (J. Countryman Press, 1998); and Henri Nouwen, *The Inner Voice of Love* (Doubleday, 1996). Where specific phrases spoke to me, I have reproduced those words in italics in my field notes, sometimes modifying them to fully integrate their wisdom with my experiences in those moments.

In the list below, citations from *Daily Light* (DL) reflect the fact that the source is organized by calendar date instead of page number. Citations from *Inner Voice of Love* (IV) include the headings Nouwen assigned to the entries in his "secret journal" along with the page number.

July:
DL: July 31

August:
DL: August 9, 14, 15, 19, 23, 25, 30

September:

DL: September 3, 4, 6, 8, 9, 10, 11, 14, 17, 25, 26, 27

IV: September 18 - *For Now, Hide Your Treasure* (p. 111-112)

IV: September 29 - *Let Your Lion Lie Down with Your Lamb* (p. 78-79)

October:

DL: October 2, 3, 10, 11, 18, 19, 20

IV: October 5 - *For Now, Hide Your Treasure* (p. 111-112)

IV: October 18 - *Claim Your Unique Presence in Your Community* (p. 67)

November:

DL: November 4, 11

ABOUT THE AUTHOR

Jennifer Pirecki is a healing educator, author, and licensed marriage and family therapist. Within her private therapy practice of twenty-four years, Jennifer guides clients and trains therapists in her integrative program of healing and spiritual wholeness. She resides in Franklin, Tennessee, with Bruno, her husband of thirty years, and their litter of rescue cats. *The Endless Abiding: Field Notes from the Journey Within* joins literary siblings *Reckoning With Dust* and *Anthroprose*.

    www.jenniferpirecki.com
    IG: @ jennifer.pirecki
    FB: jennifer pirecki author

www.ingramcontent.com/pod-product-compliance
Lightning Source LLC
Chambersburg PA
CBHW020735020526
44118CB00033B/649